THE ENTREPRENEURIAL SPIRIT

Fortune reported that some employees of Merrill Lynch's New York office were so incensed at its poor mailroom service a few years ago that they sent interoffice mail via Federal Express. Wrote *Fortune*, "Memos were whisked from floor to floor via Memphis."

IT SEEMED LIKE A GOOD IDEA AT THE TIME

Two escaped convicts were arrested hours after their escape from England's Dartmoor Prison at a house less than a mile away. They had stopped for afternoon tea.

LEAST COMPETENT CRIMINALS

Eugene "Butch" Flenough, Jr., was arrested in Austin, Texas, for robbery of a pizza restaurant after employees identified him. To hide his face during the robbery, Flenough wore a motorcycle helmet (which had "Butch" and "Eugene Flenough, Jr." written on it).

ODD ENDINGS

Charles W. Doak, owner of the Wilson Candy Company in Rocky Mount, North Carolina, was killed during a robbery after being hit on the head several times by a 9-pound, 2½-foot candy cane.

CHUCK SHEPHERD teaches law and regulation at the George Washington University business school and writes the weekly "News of the Weird" feature, which appears in several dozen daily and weekly newspapers. JOHN J. KOHUT is a political analyst for a large corporation in Washington, D.C. ROLAND SWEET is a magazine editor and a regular contributor of weird news to several alternative newspapers.

CHUCK SHEPHERD,
JOHN J. KOHUT,
& ROLAND SWEET

•••••••••••••••••••••••••••••••

BEYOND NEWS OF THE WEIRD

•••••••••••••••••••••••••••••••

A PLUME BOOK

PLUME
Published by the Penguin Group
Penguin Books USA Inc., 375 Hudson Street,
New York, New York 10014, U.S.A.
Penguin Books Ltd, 27 Wrights Lane, London W8 5TZ, England
Penguin Books Australia Ltd, Ringwood, Victoria, Australia
Penguin Books Canada Ltd, 10 Alcorn Avenue,
Toronto, Ontario, Canada M4V 3B2
Penguin Books (N.Z.) Ltd, 182–190 Wairau Road,
Auckland 10, New Zealand

Penguin Books Ltd, Registered Offices:
Harmondsworth, Middlesex, England

Published by Plume, an imprint of New American Library,
a division of Penguin Books USA Inc.

First Printing, October, 1991
10 9 8 7 6 5 4

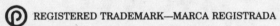 REGISTERED TRADEMARK—MARCA REGISTRADA

LIBRARY OF CONGRESS CATALOGING IN PUBLICATION DATA

Shepherd, Chuck.
  Beyond news of the weird / Chuck Shepherd, John J. Kohut &
Roland Sweet.
    p. cm.
  Included bibliographical references.
  ISBN 0-452-26716-1
  1. Curiosities and wonders—United States—Humor. 2. Curio-
sities and wonders—United States—Anecdotes. 3. United
States—History, Local—Humor. 4. United States—History,
Local—Anecdotes.
I. Kohut, John J. II. Sweet, Roland. III. Title.
E179.S5475 1991
973—dc20   *91-18367*
                                                     CIP

Printed in the United States of America
Set in New Century Schoolbook
Designed by Steven N. Stathakis

BOOKS ARE AVAILABLE AT QUANTITY DISCOUNTS WHEN USED TO PRO-
MOTE PRODUCTS OR SERVICES. FOR INFORMATION PLEASE WRITE TO
PREMIUM MARKETING DIVISION, PENGUIN BOOKS USA INC., 375 HUD-
SON STREET, NEW YORK, NEW YORK 10014.

CONTENTS

ACKNOWLEDGMENTS

We are most grateful to Denis Wade, whose breathtaking collection from the *San Francisco Chronicle* helped us fill many holes in our collections; to the maniac Ivan Katz, whose three-volume *Eunuchs Convene in India* was an inspiration to us throughout our preparation of this manuscript; and to Harry Farkas, whose annual *Journal of Bizarre Occurrences and Ridiculous Deaths* sets tough standards for us.

We would also like to thank those friends who made a special contribution to this new volume of strangeness. They are Jim White (Chief Black Mountain Correspondent), Jamie Moore and Bill Harris (Pacific Northwest Lookouts), John Orr, Lisa Reed, Roxanne Scott, Attila, Chris DeVries, Rex Wingerter, Kerry Loring, Little Gregory, Big Gregory, Heidi Bunes, Grey Scheer, Scott Scheer, P.I., David Landsidle, Donald Smith, Molly and Folly, Rich Pawlak, Debbie and John, Ginny Scheer, Peter Favini, Charlie Carr, Pansy,

Mr. Eagan's, Jonathan Horlick, MacTavish, Susan Scheer, Julian Scheer, Libby Bunn, the Walkers, Magdalen Kohut, Joe Kohut, Jake Geesing, SandwichHead (for cutting and pasting), Cujo, and always, 'Lissa. Special thanks to Matt Sartwell, Gail Ross, and Elizabeth Outka.

Thanks also to Mike Greenstein, Steve Moss, Margaret Engle, L. Richard "Rick" Mariani, Kihm Winship, and Theodora Tilton.

We are grateful to collectors who sent us classic/ inspirational clippings, including: Ed Aderer, Russell Ash, Gloria Bartek, Patrick Bishop, Mark Borinsky, Keith Clark, John Connell, Karl Engle (*The Daily Blab*), Bob Fogelnest, Jim Garrett, Jonathan Ginsburg, Stephen Gross, Edward Kimball, Brian Kirkpatrick, Steven Lauria, Stephen Lee, Robin Levitt, Everett Long, John Morris (*Copyright Infringement Quarterly*), Leonard Pape, Louis Phillips, Jason Renaud, Susan Schock, David Shimm, Thomas Slone, Neal Thompson, Francis Toldi, Roy Villa, Tom Wendt, Willy Werby, Warren Woessner, William C. Young, and Patricia Zizzamia.

Weird news clippers certainly headed for the hall of fame include Kenneth Anger, Gaal Shepherd Crowl, Linda Cunningham, Paul R. Jones II, Matt Mirapaul, the sainted Chip Rogers, Jim Sweeney, Pat Washburn, and especially Christine Van Lenten.

Only a half step behind them are some of North America's foremost weird-finders, including Linda Anderson, Jean Arnold, Tom Arnold, Suzanne Artemieff, Toni Ax, Suzi Baker, Jenny Beatty, Jon Beaupre, John Freeman Blake, Randle Brashear, Dan Brennan, Margo Brown, Trapper Byrne, Boyd Campbell, Anne Chavre, Doral Chenoweth, Lawrence Clark,

Stephanie Clipper, Michael Colpitts, Eddie Cress, Ruth Czirr, Nancy Debevoise, Tim Dorr, Bill Dowling, David Durfee, Kristi Edon, Geoffrey Egan, Robert Eland Dave Elgin, Kevin Elm, Jamie Elvebak, Margot Emery, Ernie Englander, Paul Evans, Fred Fox, Sam Gaines, Mark Garrett, Leslie Goodman-Malamuth, Joe Goulden, Marilyn Green, Glenn Greenwood, Charles Gritzner, Robert Haines, Libby Hatch, Steven Hill, Dorothy John, Chuck Jones, Herb Jue, Jim Kane, Emory Kimbrough, W. Kirchmeir, Richard Kline, Jane Kochersperger, Frederick Kopec, Mike Kosmatka, Robert Lacy, Andrew Laing, Sylvia Lee, David Leiker, J. Michael Lenninger, Harry Lewis, Mike Lewyn, Cheryl Liles, Wendy Lima, Myra Linden, Pete Lineberger, Fred Lipton, Dick Luke, Ross Mackenzie, Steve Magnuson, Walter Maiser, Tim Maloney, Bob Manley, Diane Marcus, Bob Maslow, Mark Mason, Aurlie McCrea, Jim McNally, David Menconi, Paul Miller, Brian Minsker, Terry Murphy, Kenneth Nahigian, Ray Nelke, Tom Nelson, Marci Novak, S. N. Ordahl, Paul Parker, Matt Paust, John Pell, John Peterson, Edward O. Phillips, Linda Phillips, Jerry Pohlen, Yvonne Pover, Debbie Prost, John Ray, Rollo Rayjaway, Barbara Kate Repa, David Ronin, Saul Rosenberg, Jay Russell, Jimmy Schmidt, Joe Schwind, Sherry Schurhammer, Bob Sellers, C. C. Shepherd, Ruby Shepherd, Paul Sieveking, Peter Smagorinsky, J. B. Smetana, Michael Smith, Martin Avery Snyder, Allan Spitzer, Milford Sprecher, Phil Sprick, Debby Stirling, Maurice Suhre, Maurine Taylor, Tony Tellier, Lang Thompson, Susie Thompson, Ed Toler, Marty Turnauer, Elizabeth Vantine, John Vogl, Mike Vogl, Kevin Walsh, Will Ward, Debbie Weeter, Elaine Weiss, Tracy Westen,

Brian Wilson, Everett Wittmer, Elliot Woodward, Bill Woodyard, Tim Wyatt, and Susan Zurcher.

Further thanks go to Jack Shafer; Lee Salem, Bob Duffy, and Sue Roush; Ted Hornbein, Lisa Johnson, and Ellen Haug; and J. J. Yore.

And we still think John Bendel and Jay Leno give us more pleasure (by reporting great things we missed) than anxiety (by taking sales away from us with their great books).

INTRODUCTION

● ●

Dear Reader,

Strange days indeed. Are things really getting weirder or is it just us? Consider if you will, just a bit of the new batch ... a candy cane club, Marilyn Monroe's bed, "Stoneman," nail gun dangers, product quality control in China, chess with the dead (they're not very good players), dental floss escape rope, owl vomit, fishing with dynamite, the "Happy Swordsman Executioner," so many people with chainsaws, panty bandits, the nude lawn mower, horny dolphins, horseplay at a nuclear power plant, missing brains, French château doghouses, a man who thinks he's a cat, toe sucking, the homemade artificial inseminator, underground European people factories (and what's wrong with that?), a Lyndon Johnson cult, 7,000 dead King Penguins, a plane downed by falling fish, the "bus buff," 250,000 stuffed animals, "The Burper," Corey Feldman, "Blast Art," God continues telling people to do the strangest things, terrorists bomb a nudist camp, "scrotum on the head," ... (is your pulse racing yet?) ... All this and so much more in one tidy little tome. We could have gone further, but we've determined that about six hundred of these reports is the maximum the average human brain can tolerate in a given sitting. Otherwise your head would explode.

Here we are with book three as the approaching millenium begins to breathe hot and heavy on our necks. From the look of our mail, your interest in these subjects is mushrooming. Thanks for everything you've sent. We've loved every weird article and letter you've mailed, dear reader. Please, don't stop. You make going to the mailbox each day an adventure. It gives us the same feeling we get watching *The Exorcist*—whenever the camera approaches the closed door to Linda Blair's bedroom. Go ahead. Make our heads shake one more time. Send all your weird news clips (dated and showing the source, please) to:

Strange News
P.O. Box 25682
Washington, D.C. 20007

Until next time, remember, never light a match to check a gas leak, don't sit on glass tables, refrain from eating zoo animals, don't marry anyone claiming to be Joe Montana, and never, never try to stop a train using your psychic powers. Keep your heads down, keep watching the skies, and stay out of the woods at night.

CHUCK SHEPHERD
JOHN J. KOHUT
ROLAND SWEET
WASHINGTON, D.C.
APRIL 1991

2

THE LITIGIOUS SOCIETY

● ●

THE NEW YORK COURT OF AP-
peals finally rejected an appeal against a tennis tournament sponsor from the family of tennis umpire
Richard Wertheim. Wertheim was killed during the
1983 tournament when he fractured his skull after
collapsing in pain onto the hard court surface after
having been struck in the testicles by a ball hit by
Stefan Edberg.

A NEW JERSEY APPEALS COURT
refused to block a lawsuit filed by Vincent Vecere
against Trump Castle Hotel and Casino for negligence. Vecere said the hotel was responsible when he
swung his hand back (while shaking dice) and hit a
post on the craps table.

THE VIRGINIA SUPREME COURT

upheld a $150,000 jury verdict to Martha J. Love for back injuries she suffered when she fell off a loose toilet seat in a Richmond office building. A lower court judge had overruled the verdict, saying the woman was automatically at fault, but the high court said not necessarily, especially since the seat "appeared to be positioned properly on the toilet (when she sat down)."

....

A SAN FRANCISCO WOMAN WAS

awarded $350,000 by a jury against the city for injuries sustained when she fell in a public park. She had been drinking, took a taxi home, and got the driver to stop en route so she could answer a call of nature in a clump of bushes at the edge of the park. She lost her balance, tumbled down a hill that was obscured by bushes, and suffered major injuries.

....

OCIE MCCLURE, TWENTY-FOUR,

serving eight years for a street robbery in San Francisco, filed a $5 million lawsuit against the cab driver who apprehended him. The driver had pinned McClure against a wall with his taxi, damaging McClure's leg.

....

ST. PAUL, MINNESOTA, BANK

President Michael Brennan filed a $50,000 lawsuit

against the city and a construction company for a mishap in his bank's restroom. The construction company had shut off a sewer line without notifying the bank, and when Brennan flushed, he was suddenly washed out with "200 to 300 gallons" of raw sewage. The company offered only to buy him a new suit.

....

RABBI LORING J. FRANK WAS

sued in Fort Lauderdale by two lawyers because he had been ninety minutes late in performing their wedding in 1988. Christine and Russell Adler claimed that Frank's delay allowed guests to run up a bar bill, caused Russell's back condition to flare up, and led guests to gossip about whether the marriage was in trouble. The Adlers thought those problems were worth $130,000—seven times the cost of the wedding.

....

MICHAEL RUBIN, A LOS ANGELES

lawyer specializing in personal injury cases, filed a $2 million lawsuit against his neighbor, tax lawyer Kenneth Schild, whose basketball made too much noise bouncing on his backyard court. Schild said Rubin had threatened to trespass to forcibly prevent him from playing and once squirted Schild and his son with a hose to get them to stop.

....

SINCE AROUND 1970, A WOMAN

(unidentified in a newspaper story) has been filing

papers in Jefferson County (Birmingham), Alabama, probate court complaining about the government's illegal compiling of information on people. She identifies herself in each paper by name, address, social security number, and (in large, upper-case letters) "VIRGIN!"

···

ENDING LITIGATION THAT BEGAN

in 1986, the U.S. Court of Appeals in California upheld a trial court's award of $8,000 to an airline coach passenger from a first-class passenger who had roughed her up. The defendant, a Presbyterian church deacon, got upset when she wouldn't let him break in front of her to use the first-class lavatory.

···

GLORIA SYKES, IN HER MID-

twenties at the time, filed a $500,000 lawsuit for a 1964 cable car accident. Sykes claimed that, before the accident, she was extremely religious and straitlaced, but that, as a result of the accident, she acquired an obsession for "contact with a body that results in a desire for sexual contact."

···

THE ENTREPRE-NEURIAL SPIRIT

• •

A FIFTY-FOUR-YEAR-OLD ITALIAN schoolteacher was arrested for trying to sell as many as seven hundred homemade videotapes of couples engaged in extramarital sex. The teacher was popular in his small town of Striano for offering his home for trysts, but he would secretly tape the sessions and offer them for sale in Naples, hoping the participants would not find out.

....

BILL R. CLARK, SIXTY-ONE, OF Jonesboro, Arkansas, was issued a patent for his invention that embosses numbers on the heels of socks to help identify them when they come out of the dryer, saving the owner the time needed to match them up.

....

IN A PRICE WAR ON BANANAS

between Twin Valu and Food 4 Less in Cuyahoga Falls, Ohio, which started at 50 cents per pound, the competitors repeatedly lowered the prices until Twin Valu began giving bananas away for free. Food 4 Less then matched that price but began taping pennies to each bunch.

....

A JAPANESE COMPANY PAID

$60,300 at an auction in 1989 in Hohokus, New Jersey, for the marital bed of Joe DiMaggio and Marilyn Monroe.

....

HAMMACHER SCHLEMMER OFFERED

the "French Château Doghouse" in 1989 for $2,950, not counting such options as a marble floor and down-filled cushions.

....

THE PHILIPPINE BROADCASTERS'

Association fined station ABS-CBN $11,600 for a 1988 incident in which it sandwiched the 91-second-long Mike Tyson–Michael Spinks boxing match with one hour of commercials.

....

THE CALIFORNIA SUPREME COURT

ruled that cancer patient John Moore was entitled to

profit from the enlarged, cancerous spleen that was removed by operation in 1976. After the operation, doctors used the spleen to develop anticancer drugs, and Moore figured the potential profit from those drugs was more than $3 billion.

....

JUAN CORDOVA AND JOSE GUZ-
man were arrested in Lima, Peru, for fraud. They had allegedly gathered used condoms from a lover's lane beach, then washed and resold them as new.

....

IN INDIA, MOLOY KUNDU, THIRTY-
two, and his wife, Tapati, twenty-seven, reported that each had sold a kidney to enable them to purchase a desktop publishing machine so that they could resume issuing the weekly newspaper *Bela*, for which no other financing could be found.

....

FORTUNE REPORTED IN 1988 THAT
some employees of Merrill Lynch's New York office were so incensed at its poor mailroom service a few years ago that they sent interoffice mail via Federal Express. Wrote *Fortune*, "Memos were whisked from floor to floor via Memphis."

....

FETISHES
ON PARADE
....

AN FBI INVESTIGATION INTO IN-terstate trafficking by diaper fetishists resulted in the arrests of five men belonging to the Diaper Pail Foundation, which publishes a newsletter and information exchange for members. A Madison, Wisconsin, man arrested for possession of child pornography was found inside a van taking pictures of a child who was defecating into diapers. The man had offered himself to the child's parents as a free-lance toilet trainer.

....

GRANT OLIVER, TWENTY-FIVE, was arrested in Torquay, England, in 1989 when police spotted him punching and yelling at someone on the street. On closer inspection, police discovered the victim was a blow-up doll but jailed Oliver anyway for disturbing the peace.

....

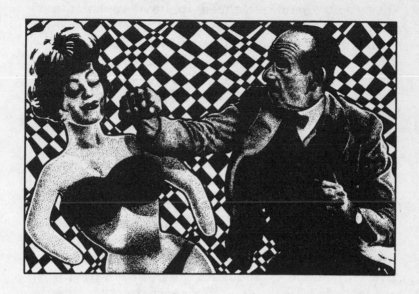

THE JASPER, TEXAS, PANTY

bandit (not related to the Tempe, Arizona, panty bandit reported in *More News of the Weird*) was arrested after an eleven-month reign. The investigation had been hampered by several victims' reluctance to report details of the crime to police. Said the sheriff, "People don't hold to nobody breaking into their homes and trifling with their undergarments."

YET ANOTHER PANTY BANDIT

mentioned in *More News of the Weird*, the Salt Lake City panty bandit, claimed to have repented religiously in 1990, as fourteen of his victims received their underwear back in the mail with a badly spelled note from the thief, apologizing. However, one of the victims received $12 cash instead of her underwear, with a note reading, "I like these. I'm not sending them back." The thief had apparently kept thorough records matching the panty owners and their garments.

....

ILLINOIS AUTHORITIES CHARGED

William Grove, thirty-three, a business professor at Loras College in Dubuque, with having stolen shoes from students at universities in two states over a five-year period by snatching them in libraries when students left their tables for short, barefoot breaks. Grove told police he donated the shoes to the homeless, but police found eighty pairs in his apartment. At around the same time, a rash of shoe thefts (one shoe at a time) was plaguing the Boston Public Library.

....

LITTLE ROCK, ARKANSAS, POLICE

charged Michael Wyatt, twenty-nine, with assault after he pushed a woman to the ground, took off her shoes and socks, and began sucking her toes. Several other victims identified him as a "podiatry student" who had met them at a shoe store and, said a police detective later, "Next thing you know, he'd have a toe in his mouth." Police suspected Wyatt right away because he had been arrested on similar charges several years ago (see *News of the Weird*, p. 134) but was released when he agreed to seek therapy.

....

ATHERTON, CALIFORNIA, NEU-

rologist Robert Bruce Spertell, forty, was arrested in a Palo Alto motel in 1989 and charged with paying a fifteen-year-old girl for sex. However, the "sex" appeared limited to having the girl tie him up and pelt him with eggs, chocolate syrup, and flour while he was dressed in a garter belt and nylons. After the story broke, at least twenty-five women notified police that they, too, had been propositioned by Spertell for similar acts. Spertell said he had been having trouble with "impulse control."

....

LEE WARRICK, THIRTY-NINE, WAS

arrested at the Mile Hi Flea Market in Denver for allegedly photographing women by pointing a wrist-mounted video camera under their skirts. Police said forty to fifty women were photographed and that Warrick was a suspect in similar incidents in Boulder and Chicago. Police said Warrick would find a target, get as close as possible, then appear to kneel down and look for something while the camera was rolling.

....

CHARLES EDWARD PADGETT,

forty-nine, was sentenced to fifteen years in prison

for a 1986 attempted sexual assault in San Antonio. According to testimony, Padgett had gone to the home of a woman he knew slightly, pulled a gun, ordered her to undress and to stand with her back to him, and then to reach behind her and, while conversing with him, to fondle a large cucumber that he had stuffed into his pocket.

LEAST COMPETENT CRIMINALS

• •

IN ORLANDO, FLORIDA, JOSEPH T. Hill was convicted of counterfeiting and faced up to twenty years in prison. His work included printing several million Polish zlotys, worth only about $300. Said a Secret Service agent, "He could have printed a boxcar full of them and not have enough to buy an expensive suit." Hill paid $19,000 for the machine to print the zlotys.

• •

FROM THE *WICHITA EAGLE* CRIME column, April 11, 1990: A man walked into a gas station, laid $2 on the counter for cigarettes, and while the attendant turned to get the cigarettes, the man reached into the cash register, took the entire paper contents, and fled. The attendant told police there was a $1 bill on top of the paper compartment, and only several scraps of paper underneath. Meanwhile, the man left the $2 on the counter.

....

POLICE ARRESTED KENNETH LANG,

thirty-two, for robbery of a 7-Eleven in Old Orchard Beach, Maine. Lang had entered the store in a black nylon mask but took it off when he realized he couldn't see. After he forced the clerk to put money in a paper bag, the bag broke, sending coins all over the floor. Lang ordered the clerk to kneel down and help him pick them up. Then, while the two argued about whether the store safe could be opened, Lang ordered the clerk to wait on customers who were coming to the register with their purchases. When the clerk complained that Lang had taken all his coins, Lang several times fished around in his bag to make change. When Lang finally began his getaway, he inadvertently kept turning right and so arrived again in front of the store, where he was arrested.

....

THOMAS LEE JONES, TWENTY-

four, was arrested for robbing a Santa Barbara, California, restaurant with a note threatening "to shot" [sic] employees. Police set up a roadblock asking people who fit Jones's description to spell "shoot" and soon apprehended Jones.

....

DRUG-POSSESSION DEFENDANT

Christopher Plovie, on trial in 1990 in Pontiac, Michigan, claimed that he had been searched without a warrant. The prosecutor said the officer didn't need a warrant because a "bulge" in Plovie's jacket could have been a gun. Nonsense, said Plovie, who happened to be wearing the same jacket that day. He handed it over so the judge could see that its material did not make bulges. The judge discovered a packet of cocaine in the pocket.

....

PORTSMOUTH, RHODE ISLAND,

police charged Gregory Rosa, twenty-five, with a string of vending machine robberies after he inexplicably fled from police when they spotted him loitering around a vending machine. Police were pretty sure they had their man when Rosa later tried to post bail using $400 in coins.

....

DAVID POSMAN, THIRTY-THREE,

was arrested in 1989 in Providence, Rhode Island, after allegedly knocking out an armored-car driver and stealing the closest four bags of money. The closest four bags were coins—each containing only pennies and weighing thirty pounds each, slowing him to a stagger during his getaway so that police officers easily jumped him from behind.

....

17

EUGENE "BUTCH" FLENOUGH,

Jr., was arrested in Austin, Texas, for robbery of a pizza restaurant after employees identified him. To hide his face during the robbery, Flenough wore a motorcycle helmet (which had "Butch" and "Eugene Flenough, Jr." written on it).

....

UNIVERSITY OF CINCINNATI GRAD-

uate student Tajiwder Brar, twenty-seven, was charged with arson in 1989 after allegedly setting fire to seven racks that displayed the campus newspaper. Police said he was upset that a $90 ad he had placed to sell his book, *The Emotional Generator*, had brought no response at all. The ad contained no information on how to obtain the book and contained only this cryptic description of its contents: "In the U.S.A., in the East, about the philosophy of your life on this planet only."

....

KOUROSH BAKHTIARI, TWENTY-

seven, was arrested for masterminding a three-man escape from a New York City correctional center, in which he meticulously braided over fifteen rolls of unwaxed dental floss to make a rope strong enough to support a 190-pound man. However, he had neglected to plan for gloves; the floss so abraded his hands he had to be hospitalized with severed tendons and ligaments.

....

TWO MEN, AGED SIXTEEN AND

eighteen, after an attempted burglary in Larkspur, California, in 1989, scaled a chain-link fence outside town to evade police who were following them, only to discover later that the fence was the outer perimenter of San Quentin Prison, where guards soon arrested them.

....

KEVIN L. JONES, TWENTY, WAS

arrested in Richmond, Virginia, after walking into a police station to post bail for a friend. He and his girlfriend stared a little too long at the wanted poster featuring his name and photograph, drawing the attention of officers.

....

TWO INMATES AT THE LOGAN

County, Utah, jail were charged with various crimes in 1990 after having made their third foray of the evening from the jail (this time to set a fire in the sheriff's office evidence room). They first escaped through a crawl hole to get beer from the wife of one of the three, then returned to jail. A few minutes later, they left to steal weapons and get more beer, then returned. After their third adventure, an officer noticed empty beer cans outside the office door.

....

A FIVE-BLOCK AREA OF SOUTH

Philadelphia was hot with a one-day crime wave in

1984, when, an unarmed man unsuccessfully tried to hold up four banks and a check-cashing store in a twenty-minute span. According to detective Pat Laurenzi, "At each place, when he passed his note [which included the words thank you and please], he was turned down or they panicked, and he just turned around and walked out."

....

GOVERNMENT IN ACTION

....

IN 1984, WALTER DEBOW WON A

judgment for $3.4 million in damages against the city of East Saint Louis, Illinois, for a wrongful beating he suffered while in city jail, but he was unable to collect, as the city had been bankrupt. In 1990, as compensation, DeBow was given title to the city's main municipal building and its 220-acre industrial park.

....

CZECHOSLAVAKIA'S NEW GOVERN-

ment scheduled a striptease dance show for foreign visitors in Prague in 1989 but then discovered the previous government had authorized only two women in the entire country to be stripteasers. One was located, but she was out of practice and tired after only a few minutes.

....

POLICE IN GRANADA HILLS, CAL-

ifornia, arrested five Los Angeles housewives, members of a bowling league, who were betting a couple of dollars a week in their matches. Police learned of the bets through the tip of a disgruntled former member, and two vice squad officers staked out the bowling alley for two hours, watching $8 change hands.

THE GOVERNMENT OF CHINA EX-

ecuted twelve male and six female factory managers by firing squad at a refrigerator plant just outside Beijing in 1989 because the poor quality of their products constituted "unpardonable crimes against the people of China." Customers had complained for years about having to wait for refrigerators that were unusable when delivered.

THE STATE OF CALIFORNIA TOOK

four years, twenty-five drafts, and $600,000, but finally produced its "Wellness Guide" giving advice on proper living habits. Among the guidelines for parents: "Don't beat, starve, or lock up your kids." Among the other advice: "Don't buy something you can't afford." And: "If you are sexually active and don't want to make a baby, you may want to use birth control."

WASHINGTON STATE SENATOR

Jim West proposed in 1989 to make it illegal for

couples under eighteen to engage in "heavy petting,"
but the bill was killed in committee the next year.

....

THE ILLINOIS DEPARTMENT OF

Conservation created a program, with $180,000 from
the legislature, to study the contents of owl vomit to
determine what owls eat during different seasons.

....

HEALTH SERVICES LEGISLATION

in the Florida House of Representatives was voted
down in 1990, with the deciding vote cast by Representative Mike Langton's son, twelve, who was fool-
ing around with the electronic vote machine on his
father's desk on the floor of the House. Representative Langton said he personally would have voted yes
but had stepped away to make a phone call when the
vote came up, leaving his son alone.

....

JOSEPH C. CLEMONS, TWENTY-

six, housed in a courthouse cell in Fredericksburg,
Virginia, pending a court appearance for breaking
into a motel, pried open the cell door, walked down a
hallway and past guards at the front door, and escaped, all while wearing leg irons. (He was not discovered missing until a local citizen called police to report
a man walking down the street wearing shackles.)

....

AFTER MUCH CRITICISM IN 1990,

the Naples, Florida, Police Department canceled a highly touted campaign against drug dealers. The department, which has one black officer (out of seventy-five), had dressed undercover white officers in black-face and colorful clothes because, said one official, "sales are made predominantly by blacks."

....

WHEN THE ONLY LAW ENFORCE-

ment officer in Arcade, Georgia, Sid Glenn, was arrested for attempted burglary, in 1989, an *Atlanta Journal* reporter called the Arcade police department to find out who had arrested Glenn. No one answered.

....

COMPELLING
EXPLANATIONS

· ·

THE OKLAHOMA DEPARTMENT OF
Human Services began in 1990 to publish a monthly
list of the worst excuses received for nonpayment of
child support. Among the first winners: "I can't afford
to pay child support [because] I've got to pay my cable
TV bill"; "We only had sex one time [therefore] I couldn't
be the father"; and "I will not allow my ex-wife to get
rich on my money [$25 a week]."

· ·

LOUISIANA STATE REPRESENTA-
tive Carl Gunter, opposing an exception to an antiabortion bill for victims of incest: "Inbreeding is how
we get championship horses."

· ·

KATHY OLIVER, DIRECTOR OF A

Portland, Oregon, drug treatment program, commenting on the success of giving free, clean needles to intravenous (IV) drug users: "It proves that IV drug users are . . . willing to go out of their way to protect their health."

....

A CAIRO NEWSPAPER REPORTED

that Mohammed El Mahdi Essa, thirty-eight, was arrested in a sting operation for selling his son, three, to raise about $700 to buy a videocassette recorder. Essa told police he was forced to do it because of his honesty. Said he, "I have never stolen in my life."

....

A SEATTLE POLICE OFFICER SAID

a sixty-eight-year-old woman arrested for shoplifting four packs of cigarettes blamed the episode on Judge Wapner of *The People's Court*. She said she was driven to experiment after hearing the judge tell talk-show host Pat Sajak that "everybody steals, at least once in their life."

....

A TWENTY-YEAR-OLD MAN IN

Columbia, Missouri, complained that his driver's license was wrongfully revoked under a youth statute—based on the state's antiabortion law. His lawyer reasoned that if life begins at conception and not at birth, the accused man was twenty-one, not twenty, when arrested for drunk driving and therefore subject to the more lenient adult law.

....

NEWSPAPERS IN NAPLES, ITALY,

reported that, in a lawsuit against an insurance company, a couple had blamed the woman's pregnancy on an automobile accident. She claimed that, while the couple was making out in a car in a notorious lover's lane, another car rammed their car from behind, causing the couple to "lose control" and be unable to avoid the insemination.

....

A TWENTY-EIGHT-YEAR-OLD IN-

dustrial engineer was fired from his job in Cookeville, Tennessee, after an incident in which he was charged with indecent exposure (a charge that was later dropped). He was apprehended outdoors at a mall, stark naked. His explanation was that his car had broken down and, despite a heavy rainstorm, he needed to get underneath the car to see what was wrong. He was afraid of muddying the seat covers so he took off his clothes—including underwear and socks—and laid them across the seat.

....

BRUCE F. HUNT, TWENTY-SEVEN,

beat a DWI rap in Auburn, New York, when the jury accepted Hunt's testimony that he had swerved across the center line in a 1986 incident not because of intoxication but because he was having oral sex performed on him while driving.

. . . .

IN AN INTERVIEW ON ESPN IN

1989, football star Eric Dickerson said he wasn't ready for marriage. "I'm not the best-looking guy, and I don't want an ugly wife because we will have ugly kids, no doubt. My mother even said, 'Please don't have an ugly wife and make ugly babies.' "

. . . .

GREGORY FENSOM, THIRTY-

two, was fired by the RE/MAX real estate office in Independence, Missouri, after he led five people to a sale house listed with his office and staged a 3 A.M. party with drinking and loud TV. Fensom did not know that the owner had not yet vacated the house, and when she appeared from her bedroom, Fensom said, "I'm the realtor, and I'm showing the house."

. . . .

A MAN USING AN OUTHOUSE

near Lawrence, Kansas, said he lost his footing while trying to retrieve his wallet, which had fallen through the floorboards. He fell in and had to spend seven hours in three feet of muck before being rescued. Douglas County Sheriff Loren Anderson described the man as unhurt "but in a pretty ugly mood."

. . . .

CHUTZPAH

....

TWO MEN WHO HAD COME TO court in Waterbury, Connecticut, to answer assault and weapons charges were arrested when they allegedly tried to steal two cheap rugs on their way out of the courtroom. Three months later, someone, for the fifth time, stole the microwave oven out of a jury room in a courthouse in San Antonio, Texas.

....

IN 1985, A FLORIDA CIRCUIT judge denied the motion of Gary Taylor, charged with a drunk-driving accident that killed four people, that he be allowed to have beer in his cell while awaiting trial. Taylor's lawyer had argued that before he was jailed Taylor had the ability to consume large amounts of alcohol (he was tested at .24 level just after the accident) and still function normally, but that while in jail, that ability to tolerate alcohol was deteriorating and thus he needed the beer to keep in training.

....

IN JUNE 1990, U.S. SENATOR

Strom Thurmond requested a $25 refund from Lexington, South Carolina, for a water deposit he paid in 1938. (He was eligible for the refund because he had recently sold the property.) Asked the mayor, "How in the hell can anyone save a receipt for fifty-two years?"

....

JOHNNIE LEE JONES, TWENTY-

seven, in prison since 1985, when he stole a truck in Fort Lauderdale, Florida (even though he'd never learned to drive), and smashed it into several cars, killing a young mother, was on the verge of a large financial settlement from Broward County Prison (as this book was going to press); it wants to save the cost of a lawsuit. In his getaway from the collisions, Jones ran in front of a car and had one leg chopped off; he later filed a lawsuit charging that the prison had caused him "pain and suffering" because of its lack of facilities to help his recuperation. The prison offered evidence that Jones was a disruptive prisoner, having urinated on a fellow prisoner and beaten another with his artificial leg.

....

THE REVEREND W. N. OTWELL,

Texas gubernatorial candidate in 1990, declared that

the floods and other natural disasters that had bedeviled Texas since 1986 were the Lord's retribution for all the attacks on Otwell. Said Otwell, "We've been keeping stats on this."

SILVIA MATOS LEFT NEW YORK

City without a trace shortly before officials cracked down on her for 2,800 unpaid parking tickets (over a 38-month period, an average of 2.5 per day), totaling $171,000 in fines. She had registered her car at 19 addresses with 36 different license plates.

A THIRTY-EIGHT-YEAR-OLD ROB-

bery victim in Salt Lake City told police he could not recognize the robber's face, but that he could identify him by his cologne and by "holding his genitals." The two men apparently were sitting in a car fondling each other when one took the other's watch and fled.

DENISE AND JEFFREY LAGRIMAS,

who were hosting a neighborhood-watch meeting in their Oroville, California, home, were arrested during the meeting after a neighbor spotted her stolen TV set in the Lagrimas home and then realized that Denise was wearing her stolen dress. Police officers giving a presentation at the meeting obtained a search warrant and found $9,000 worth of stolen goods.

GROWN-UPS

· ·

TWO DENTON, TEXAS, FATHERS

of players on a girls' soccer team became frustrated at the opponents' goalie's skill and demanded that the girl (age ten) "prove" her gender to game officials. (The men were suspended as spectators for the rest of the season.)

· ·

REDFORD, MICHIGAN, POLICE

charged Dale Roy Dietz with child abuse for ordering his child to act (as police described) "like a robot" when he was around his mother, who is Dietz's estranged wife, for the purpose of irritating her. Dietz reportedly called the nine-year-old boy daily, told him of "a mission" to rattle the mother (whom Dietz called "Fang"), and encouraged the boy not to speak or eat or obey, and to attack the mother as often as possible. Police say the calls might have permanently changed the boy's personality.

....

CRITICISM CAME TO LIGHT IN

the late 1980s about the practice of peasants working along the Yellow River south of Beijing who tradition- ally leave their infants tied inside sandbags each day while they are at work. The practice supposedly teaches obedience, keeps the child warm during winter, and allows sand to function as a diaper. Preliminary evi- dence shows babies develop more slowly if kept in sandbags.

....

FIVE MIAMI FIREFIGHTERS WERE

disciplined for hazing a visiting firefighter by tying him to a chair and playing "scrotum on the head," in which one man drops his pants and steps over the sitting victim so that his genitals graze the man's face. The practice came to light after the victim broke free and squeezed a man's testicles.

....

GROCERY STORE MANAGER AB-

dullah Shaheen was arrested in Fort Lauderdale for pulling a loaded .357 Magnum on three young girls when they came up two cents short to pay for bubble gum.

....

IN BOSSIER CITY, LOUISIANA,

Terry Polk, twenty-six, got into a dispute at a party. He challenged his adversary to settle matters with a head-butting duel, and the two banged each other several times. Polk died shortly afterward from a cerebral hemorrhage.

....

THE PILGRIM NUCLEAR POWER

plant in Massachusetts was shut down for five days during 1986 at a cost of $250,000, because of workers' horseplay. Workers had rolled up a pair of gloves and taped them tightly to simulate a ball, which had been lost during a game because of an overthrow into a backup safety tank.

....

TO DRAMATIZE HIS OPPOSITION

to a bill to ban contraceptives on school grounds, State Representative Ben McGee held up his open wallet and asked the Arkansas General Assembly, "I wonder how many of you remember being in school and having a circle in your wallet."

....

ORDER IN THE COURT

. . . .

A MILTON, FLORIDA, WOMAN
was allowed by a federal tax court to deduct travel
expenses to and from her job, a deduction not ordinar-
ily allowed. She proved that her "job" was as a blood
donor, and that the travel was the only way to get her
profit-making product to market. (However, the court
disallowed her claim for a "mineral depletion allowance" for the minerals in her blood, finding that
Congress intended that deduction only for mining
activities.)

. . . .

A JURY IN GWINNETT COUNTY,
Georgia, found Herbert Freels, twenty-four, guilty of
rape in 1989, despite his having produced a note
signed by the victim, stating, "I was not raped. I did
it under my own free will." Freels was distraught

after the verdict, claiming that he "always" has his sexual partners write such notes.

....

AS PART OF THE CONDITION OF

probation for Ronald P. Edwards, who pleaded guilty to battery in Pineville, Louisiana, Judge Joel Chaisson ordered Edwards to remove the curse Edwards had placed on him at the time of his arrest.

....

DOUG BRIGHTMOSER WAS AR-

rested in Nashville in 1990 on a neighbor's complaint that he was firing a shotgun into the air at night. Brightmoser explained in court that he was not firing to cause trouble but was shooting at a snake that was "trying to suck the nipples" of a goat in his yard. During his arraignment, Brightmoser continually answered not "Yes, Your Honor," but "Yeah, Bubba," which he later told a reporter was not a term of disrespect.

....

THE IDAHO COURT OF APPEALS

granted a partial victory in 1990 to a man charged with masturbating in a public restroom, remanding the case to the trial court to determine whether an undercover police officer had violated the man's right to privacy by peering into a restroom stall. The case is *State* v. *Dale D. Limberhand.*

....

DISTRICT JUDGE BRIGITA VOLO-

pichova, twenty-seven, of Pizen, Czechoslavakia, was disciplined by legal authorities for bringing "disgrace" to judges by entering a televised "Miss Topless" event. She came in second.

....

CONVICTED MURDERER THOMAS

Marston argued in his appeal that conflicts of interest were responsible for his 1985 conviction in Mendocino County, California. First, he submitted evidence that his attorney had fathered the child of the then-district attorney, who was allegedly hassling the father for support at the time of the trial. Then a witness informed the appeals court that the mother had told her that the real father was not the lawyer, but the judge in the case.

....

BROWARD COUNTY, FLORIDA,

Judge Paul Marko, in a 1990 divorce case, forbade Marianne Price, thirty-three, from having boyfriends over to her house because it was formerly joint property but said her husband could have the "entire [Miami] Dolphins cheerleading squad running through his apartment naked" because it was "his" apartment. Marko then advised Price to start visiting singles bars: "I've been [in them]. I'm a single man. There are all kinds of . . . guys running around in open shirts with eagles on their chests. There are great guys out there." Marko said he would order Price's house sold if she allowed a male to live there:

"I don't want her all of a sudden taking up with some nice, sweet, little blond from Norway." (Marko later apologized to Price, and several months later his decision was overturned.)

....

ORANGE COUNTY, CALIFORNIA,
Superior Court clerks discovered in 1989 that they had failed to complete the paperwork to make nearly five hundred pre-1985 divorce judgments final, thus leaving the parties still legally married. The worst-case scenario for one husband occurred after an error by an Arizona court in 1990 when Bonita Lynch was ruled one-fourth owner of her ex-husband's $2.2 million lottery jackpot because a paperwork error delayed the official divorce date eleven days, during which time he won the lottery.

....

IN 1990, ALPHONSO CALHOUN,
thirty-nine, was convicted in Cleveland of raping a twenty-seven-year-old woman who said Calhoun forced her to perform fellatio four times in exchange for drugs. Calhoun was convicted despite the fact that, after the fourth incident, the woman had bitten off Calhoun's testicles after he had passed out, and had walked off with his drugs and money. Testified Calhoun in his own behalf: "I looked down [after being jarred awake]. The pouch [of drugs and money] was gone. My scrotum was gone."

....

ON TRIAL FOR FIRST-DEGREE

murder in Tampa, Perry Taylor claimed it was second-degree at best because the victim, Geraldine Johnson Birch, had provoked him to beat her when she bit him during oral sex. To augment his testimony, Taylor presented photographs of his bite-marked penis to the jury.

....

TO SETTLE A LAWSUIT INVOLV-

ing a man who died during a construction accident in Houston, his relatives agreed to forgo their claim on $50,000 from one of the defendants, Derr Construction Company, if Derr's lawyer (who was the lawyer most disliked by the relatives) would allow them each to punch him in the face.

....

THE SPORTS PAGES

●●●●●●●●●●●●●●●●●●●●●●●●●●●●●●●●●●●●●●

A NINTH-GRADE BOY WAS SENT into intensive care in Wauwatosa, Wisconsin, after a track meet. He had just cleared the bar while pole-vaulting when a gust of wind blew him past the landing pit onto the concrete.

●●●●●●●●●●●●●●●●●●●●●●●●●●●●●●●●●●●●●

STAN FOX, WHO FINISHED LAST in the 1990 Indianapolis 500 after traveling only ten laps before a gear box problem forced him out of the race, nonetheless earned $108,000.

●●●●●●●●●●●●●●●●●●●●●●●●●●●●●●●●●●●●●

MARGARET WELDON, SEVENTY- four and legally blind, scored a hole-in-one on the seventh hole at Amelia Island (Florida) Plantation's

Long Point course in 1990. (Her husband coaches her shots.) Then, the next day, she did it again.

···

LISA LESLIE OF MORNINGSIDE

High School in Los Angeles scored 101 points in the first half of a girls' basketball game against South Torrance High but was deprived of a shot at the record of 104 when South Torrance players decided not to play the second half. During the same season, the Neah Bay High School girls team in Seattle beat American Indian Heritage. Leading at the half, 59–2, Neah Bay earned a second-half shutout, 41–0, to win, 100–2.

···

POLICE ARRESTED JOCKEY SYL-

vester Carmouche, twenty-eight, for fraud after he had "won" a 1990 race at Delta Downs in Vinton, Louisiana. He apparently had taken advantage of the dense fog that night by laying back at the starting gate while the other horses circled the track, then joining them for the stretch run, which his fresh horse won by twenty lengths (in a time thirty-two lengths better than her last performance).

···

THE ZIMBABWE FOOTBALL ASSO-

ciation banned four soccer players for life in 1989 after they urinated on the field in Harare because witch doctors told them it would ensure victory. (They lost, 2–0.)

···

RON KRAVITZ, TWENTY-TWO,

filed a lawsuit against Mickey Mantle Sports Productions, Inc., for injuries he suffered while watching the company's video on improving his base-stealing technique. He had the video on in his basement and was attempting to "beat" Tom Seaver's pick-off throw to "first base," when he crashed into a table, resulting in torn ligaments and a severed tendon.

···

AFTER HIS SCHOOL'S 76–73

loss in the Southern Conference basketball tournament in 1989, University of Tennessee-Chattanooga player Benny Green punched East Tennessee State cheerleader Jenny Worley in the face.

....

A PHILADELPHIA-AREA HIGH

school basketball coach, Cliff Kelly, angered that the other team was deliberately running up the score on him, ordered his boys to shoot at the other team's basket. Kelly's opponents got the last 39 points of the game, with 22 of them supplied by Kelly's team, in a 100–47 loss.

....

WON'T TAKE NO FOR AN ANSWER

• •

DOCTORS IN AN APRIL 1990
medical journal article reported that, of more than
1,000 people who had undergone surgery for skin cancer from 1983 to 1987, 24 percent were back to
suntanning and 38 percent of them still did not use
sunscreen. Most of the recidivists were females whose
attitude, said a doctor, "was that skin cancer was not
enough of a problem to give up a tan."

....

TRACY JAY JONES, TWENTY-
four, was sentenced to forty years in prison in Dallas
in 1989 for two robberies of an adult bookstore. During the first, he accidentally shot himself in the genitals while pocketing his gun, aborting the robbery
(but he escaped). The next night, with a homemade
bandage on the wound, he hobbled back into the same

store and completed the robbery, but two days later was arrested.

....

SEATTLE POLICE TOOK THREE
brothers (aged seven, eight, and nine) into custody for turning in a false fire alarm. During the ensuing several hours, as police tried to locate their parents, the boys disrupted station house business by yelling and screaming, stabbing each other with plastic knives, stabbing officers with the knives while they drove the boys through town looking for their house, sticking chewing gum on themselves and the squad car, locking themselves in a restroom and writing on the walls, swinging pool cues and throwing billiard balls in the station lounge, banging on their cells when they were finally locked up, and throwing metal objects at cell windows. When their father arrived, he said he had been having trouble with the boys lately.

....

INDIA'S *CHANDIGARH TRIBUNE*
reported that an unidentified farmer whose buffalo had eaten $2,000 worth of his wife's gold jewelry twelve years earlier had just recovered the cache from its belly after waiting patiently for the buffalo to die.

....

ACCORDING TO A 1989 ASSOCI-

ated Press story, residents of the primitive South Pacific island of Tanna each day still raise the U.S. flag and formally pray that Americans will return to the island to bring them the "cargo" they brought when they used the island as a staging area during World War II and the Vietnam War. Islanders built an airstrip with a bamboo "control tower," hoping to attract U.S. planes to land; they built bamboo "refrigerators," opening them each day to see if their prayers had brought the "cargo" they remember was in the refrigerators when Americans were using the island; and one cult worships Lyndon Johnson, praying to "Johnson"-brand outboard motors that were part of the U.S. cargo.

....

YOSHIKAZU HAYASHI, THIRTY-

nine, was arrested in Tokyo for harassing his former Kyoto University professor, who he believed had been responsible for Hayashi's not having been admitted to graduate school fifteen years earlier. In the intervening years, Hayashi made over 50,000 telephone calls to the professor (routinely, 10 per night from 8 P.M. to 2 A.M.), but the professor did not ask for police assistance until March 1989.

....

CAMBRIDGE, MARYLAND, PO-

lice arrested John Darcy Bradley, forty-one, on drunken-driving charges, then released him after he promised not to drive again until he sobered up. Within minutes, he was arrested again driving home (but was released once again on the same promise). Only after his third arrest a few minutes after that when he tried to drive home again was he finally jailed.

....

PROFESSIONAL CLOWN MARVIN

Matthow, fifty-six, was sentenced to probation and medical treatments in 1989 for trying to buy sex from a teenage boy in Colorado Springs. The judge gave probation even though the last time Matthow was in jail on similar charges he continued to advertise for teenage boys from his cell through magazines and newspapers.

....

COMPTON, CALIFORNIA, CITY

council member Maxcy Dean Filer, fifty-eight, again flunked the California Bar exam in 1988 and thus remained in his position as part-time clerk for one of his two attorney sons. He had flunked the bar exam twice every year since 1967. (Just as this book was going to press, Filer was notified that he passed the 1991 test.)

....

RETALIATING WHEN AN EAST DE-

troit woman halted an affair with him in order to reconcile with her husband, Eric Sanderson allegedly attached about fifty videocassettes onto wind-shields of neighbors' and the woman's relatives' cars. The videocassettes contained sexual scenes featuring the two of them. He was also accused of distributing crude cartoons, drawn by him, featuring the couple in sexual situations.

....

MEDICAL MILESTONES

· ·

IN FORT LAUDERDALE, FLORIDA,
plastic surgeon Dr. Frank Lomagistro saved the fingers of a woman who had them almost severed when her boyfriend accidentally slammed the door on them. Lomagistro attached thirty-five fat, black leeches to her fingertips so they could draw blood strongly enough from her hand down to the fingers that the blood would return to the hand in normal circulatory motion. The operation was pronounced a success.

· ·

A 1989 MEDICAL JOURNAL ARTI-
cle reported the case of a twenty-six-year-old man who has consistently for fifteen years suffered delusions that he is a cat. At seventeen, he confessed to eating small prey, to having sex with cats, to having fallen in love with a tigress in a zoo, and to having

attempted suicide when the tigress was moved to another zoo. He still dresses in tiger-striped clothes.

....

A WISCONSIN MAN WHO HAD

been in a vegetative state for eight years as a result of a traffic accident spontaneously snapped out of it in March 1990 after being given Valium in a routine dental procedure. After walking and talking for five minutes, he fell back into the state but was revived with yet another dose of Valium.

....

THE ARIZONA PRISON SYSTEM IN

the late 1980s began experimenting with "penile plethysmography," which evaluates accused sex offenders by attaching a ring that detects changes in the circumference of the penis when the subject is shown arousing objects or photographs. Officials say results help determine whether the alleged offender should be released pending trial and in what activities he may not engage.

....

ACCORDING TO AN ARTICLE IN

the *Journal of the American Medical Association*, doctors who had advised surgery on a forty-three-year-old woman to adjust a dislocated electrode in her heart pacemaker reported that the problem had been resolved without surgery. The patient's husband had held the woman upside down with her head touching the floor and had shaken her up and down violently for five minutes. X-rays revealed that the electrode was back in place.

···

IN DULUTH, MINNESOTA, CAR-

penter Lance Grangruth accidentally shot a nail an inch and a half into his head from his nail gun, tacking his cap to his head. Said Grangruth, "I didn't actually feel it go in. I tried to take my hat off, and it wouldn't come off." The nail penetrated relatively harmlessly at a crevasse between the two lobes.

···

IN A SURVEY OF FEMALE PROSTI-

tutes for a 1990 article in the *Journal of the American Medical Association*, their median number of sexual partners reported was 2,900, with a range of from 5 to 93,740.

···

A CALIFORNIA STATE MEDICAL

board sought in 1989 to revoke the license of a Canoga Park urologist, Dr. Jorge R. Burrell, who claimed to have treated five thousand patients for allergies by injecting them with a remedy that contains their own urine.

···

CALIFORNIA OFFICIALS OPENED

an investigation in 1990 into whether Dr. Charles Turner, sixty-four, had timed the birth of a baby due around midnight on New Year's Eve so that it would be Anaheim's first baby of 1990 and could appear on a prearranged segment of a live religious broadcast. The baby was delivered at fifteen seconds after midnight, at which time Turner cleaned him, stuffed him into a Christmas stocking, and ran next door to the Melodyland Christian Center, to loud applause from the show's studio audience.

....

JENNIFER CONNOR, EIGHTEEN, A

New York woman with a high hairdo, was diagnosed in 1989 with hearing loss and a "serious" ear infection. Her physician said her ears were clogged with hair spray.

....

WEIRD SCIENCE

A PAPER PRESENTED BY A VAN-
couver consulting firm at the Indoor Air '90 conference in Toronto reported that, because of household
cleaners, housewives have a 55 percent higher risk of
getting cancer than do women who work outside the
home.

EDWARD TELLER, EIGHTY-TWO,
"Father" of the hydrogen bomb, told a Rotary Club
meeting in Oakland, California, that nuclear bombs
might help prevent massive hurricanes. Detonating a
bomb in the atmosphere might alter temperatures so
that several storms, rather than one big one, are
created.

SCIENTISTS AT THE UNIVERSITY

of California–Irvine believe they have disproved the belief that limbless animals use less energy than do legged animals. Biologist Bruce Jayne and crew monitored the movements of snakes slithering on treadmills while wearing tiny oxygen masks.

....

SCIENTISTS AT MEMPHIS STATE

University announced success recently in creating a "super male" catfish with genes so strong that it will breed only males. Since males grow more quickly than females, catfish growers' business will increase.

....

A 1989 UNITED NATIONS STUDY

disclosed that more than six hundred tons of bodily waste (from six million people and two million dogs) are released onto the ground and into the air every day around Mexico City and that deforestation has eliminated much of the foliage that previously prevented the fecal dust from contaminating the city. The colonies of microorganisms are so numerous that scientists' equipment lacks the precision necessary to count them.

....

RESEARCHERS AT THE UNIVER-

sity of Nebraska enlisted expectant mothers to provide their dirty diapers so they could study the differences in bottle- and breast-fed babies. For a proper sample, students need ten dirty diapers per day for five days from forty babies.

. . . .

SURGEONS IN PHOENIX REAT-

tached a ten-year-old boy's skull to his spine during a five-hour operation following a traffic accident. Only muscle and ligaments held the head on after the accident, and even a one-millimeter movement of the head would have meant death, but doctors predicted the boy eventually would walk out of the hospital.

. . . .

A MILWAUKEE MAN IN HIS MID-

thirties lost part of his penis in a lawn mower accident, but surgeons, in a nine-hour operation, reattached it after sewing it onto his leg to keep it alive. The man said he was repairing the mower and had it up on blocks when it fell on top of him, but the city was rife with rumors of foul play by his disgruntled wife.

. . . .

THE U.S. COURT OF APPEALS IN

1989 rejected claims by two sets of parents that their constitutional rights were violated by Lafayette, Louisiana, coroner Charles Odom. The parents claimed that the corpses of their infants, who had died of "sudden infant death syndrome," were later deliberately dropped on their heads by Dr. Odom in tests (to support testimony he was giving in another case) to determine whether infants dropped from certain heights would suffer crushed skulls.

....

STANFORD UNIVERSITY RE-

searchers ended a longstanding debate among owl specialists as to which sense owls rely on most to detect food at night. In a journal article, they concluded "sight" to be most important after conducting an experiment in which owls were fitted with eyeglasses.

....

UNIVERSITY OF MIAMI MICROBI-

ologist Patricia Mertz sought volunteers with smelly feet in 1989 so she could test her hypothesis that the odor was similar to that of limburger cheese. Her researchers sniffed lots of cheese to familiarize themselves with the scent, then studied five volunteers a day for forty-eight days, at a distance of two inches.

....

PEOPLE VERY CLOSE TO THE EDGE

· ·

HOUSTON POLICE WERE IN-itially baffled as to how Robert Lutz, twenty-four, died after they found his nude, partially decomposed body, encased in yellow plastic, inside a coffin in a man's home. Then they began receiving unsolicited phone calls from men who said the reported circumstances of death resembled the practice of "mummification," which is a "major [sexual] bondage trip," said one. "After a while you get curious to see one all the way through [to death]."

· ·

FORMER ALEXANDRIA, LOUIS-iana, Mayor Edward Karst was arrested in New Orleans after reportedly threatening by mail to kill all members of the state supreme court. One letter read, "Execution is perfectly legal [if] precipitated by a

30-year [history of] character defects by government officials who failed to do their duty." Karst was suspended as a lawyer in 1983 and failed reinstatement in 1986.

....

DAVID LUSCO, FORTY-TWO, WAS

ordered to jail after his arrest for kidnapping near Moscow, Idaho. Allegedly, he had imprisoned his wife in their pickup truck, forced her to join him in disrobing, and driven off on a reckless rampage. When she escaped and donned a passerby's coat, he chased her while wearing only a hat. When a judge ordered him held for thirty days, he replied, "I'm in jail for thirty days? If I ain't crazy, I will be."

....

LOUIS LASLO, THIRTY-SEVEN,

was charged with kidnapping for an incident in 1989 in Hellertown, Pennsylvania. George Reid, thirty-eight, was trying to turn his car around in Laslo's driveway when Laslo, arriving home, drove in behind him and blocked his exit back to the road. He advanced on Reid's car, removed the keys forcibly, and allegedly told Reid to hold his nose and hum "Yankee Doodle Dandy" while tapping out the beat on his steering wheel. Then Laslo went inside to call police to arrest the "trespassers," but when police arrived, they arrested Laslo instead.

....

AFTER TWO HIRED KILLERS

failed in their task to murder the wife of Daytona Beach, Florida, pool hall owner Konstantinos Fotopoulos, a "tryout" was given to two others in 1989 (Diedre Hunt, twenty, and Mark Ramsey, nineteen). Fotopoulos, skeptical that either was strong enough for the job, persuaded Ramsey to let himself be tied to a tree so Fotopoulos could fire live rounds at his feet to test his courage. However, before he could fire the shots, Hunt, angry at Fotopoulos's chiding her that she was too weak to kill anyone, shot and killed Ramsey. Subsequently, Fotopoulos and Hunt were easily convicted of murder because Fotopoulos had set up a video camera to record the entire incident, and police were able to confiscate the tape.

....

DR. JANIS ASHLEY TOLD A SEDA-

lia, Missouri, newspaper in 1989 that she would shortly have a sex-change operation so that she could find a wife and raise a family. She had been a woman for eleven years, following her first sex change.

....

THE WIFE OF BRUNSWICK, GEOR-

gia, handyman-inventor Teddie Eli Smith, involved in a custody dispute with him over their four-year-old daughter, said that the child was conceived with a homemade artificial inseminator Smith rigged up with a bulb syringe and hair spray container. She further said that the device had been stocked with the sperm of Smith's seventeen-year-old son by a previous marriage. Smith's daughter would thus be his granddaughter, and his current wife could be called his first wife's daughter-in-law.

....

ALBERT DUCHARME, FIFTY-

eight, was convicted of bigamy in Winnipeg after police discovered his two wives when called to rescue him (a double amputee) from his locked bathroom. He explained that his wife of sixteen years, Geraldine, had threatened to leave him unless he also married her lesbian lover, Mary-Lou, so that Geraldine could be "a wife for me and a husband for [Mary-Lou]."

....

MARI LOUISE MEDACCO, SEVEN-

teen, was arrested in Muskegon, Michigan, in 1990 and charged with having tricked two high school girls into believing she was a boy and then having sex with them several times. Medacco called herself Mario, covered her chest with bandages (claiming rib injuries), engaged in sex only in the dark, and wore an artificial penis.

....

ROBERT C. JACKSON, TWENTY-

one, was arrested in Silver Spring, Maryland, for carrying a handgun, and, during a body search, police found in Jackson's rectum a brown paper bag with seventy-eight plastic packets of rock cocaine, along with a razor blade. A police sergeant told reporters, "That's a pretty large amount [to be inside a rectum]."

....

A FORMER MALE NURSE FLED

Franklin County, Ohio, in 1988 after dropping off a roll of film for developing at a local photo shop. Shop personnel notified police that the roll contained several photographs of corpses (including one that appeared to have been sexually abused) posed in various positions. Police identified the customer as an Oregon man who had been fired from one hospital job because he spent too much time with cadavers.

....

RODNEY THORP WOOD, SIXTY,

and his wife, Nancy Steffan Wood, forty-four, committed suicide shortly after pleading guilty in Eugene, Oregon, for a scheme in which they offered to pay University of Oregon male students to have sex with Nancy in hotel rooms. Rodney, a professor, had told them they would participate in a study on how mature women perform sexually and would receive an honorarium of $10 per orgasm (the student's and Nancy's). One man said he made $30 one day but was later ridiculed on campus.

....

A TWENTY-THREE-YEAR-OLD

man was arrested in 1989 in Nashville as a suspect in several "flashing" episodes in which a man wearing a woman's dress (and with an object protruding from his rear end) bent over to moon people in shopping center parking lots. The police file on the incidents is labeled "The Carrot Man."

....

A POOR CHOICE OF WORDS

MAYOR CARL E. OFFICER OF

East St. Louis, Illinois, said that he would bring his own blood supply along on a trip to Zaire so that, in case he needed a transfusion while there, he wouldn't be contaminated with "monkey blood." Officer apologized for the remark but did note that the incident gave him "international status."

FORTY-TWO-YEAR-OLD JOSEPH

A. Dickson of Albany, New York, was arrested after he allegedly tied a belt around the neck of his thirteen-year-old daughter and forced her to crawl down the street barking like a dog because she was late returning home. "I told her if you want to act like a dog, then you get down and crawl like a dog," Dickson told the court.

RANDY JEFF CHAPMAN, THIRTY-

one, of Miami, Florida, spurned his older brother's request that he take a test to determine bone-marrow compatibility for a possible transplant, even though he had the best chance of saving the leukemia victim's life. Said the younger brother, "If he dies, he dies."

....

MISSOURI LIQUOR OFFICIALS

cited Mike Tomlin, owner of Whispers nightclub in Columbia, for sending letters to University of Missouri fraternities advertising his club as the place to find "drunk, horny women."

....

LAQUITA DAVIS, MANAGER OF

the Yogi Bear Jellystone Park Camp Resort in Lake Buena Vista, Florida, said that she gave Kim Beeston, who is legless, and Brian Lemke, who is blind, their money back and asked them to leave the campsite after another camper complained that the two were putting on "a sideshow in the park." Lemke admitted walking into a few trees and Beeston said that people often stare at her when she rolls on the ground after she gets out of her wheelchair, but neither planned to leave Jellystone.

....

JAPANESE POLICE APOLOGIZED

to Pakistan after an internal police manual surfaced

in the press. The manual warned officers that Pakistanis don't bathe and that they have "a unique body stink, so they will make interrogation rooms and detention rooms stink." Along with advising officers to wash after handling Pakistanis, it also noted that "until confronted with proof, they [Pakistanis] will do nothing but lie in the name of Allah." A senior police official said, "There are some points which might invite misunderstanding, so we are going to revise it."

....

ASKED BY A GROUP OF FOURTH-
graders in 1990 what qualifications a person needed to be mayor, Bob Cox, mayor of Fort Lauderdale, Florida, said that one need only be "free, white, and 21." Cox had earlier insulted the black community by referring to the Dillard High School football team as a "tribe" when he congratulated them on a state-championship victory.

....

DERRICK JOHNSON, TWENTY-
eight, who allegedly stole food over a period of three months from a Kansas City gas station cooler while yelling "Catch me if you think you can," was shot and killed by a station clerk.

....

AFTER BEING CONVICTED ON
nine counts of perjury, former U.S. Representative Patrick Swindall of Georgia said, "I've spoken about a

number of career opportunities, and one I've got to put into the blend is a prison ministry."

....

A JUDGE IN LITCHFIELD, CON-

necticut, ruled that Arthur J. Werley would be tried for the beating death of Kimberley Labrecque. According to court documents, Labrecque was beaten after she spurned Werley's sexual advances and told him that he looked like Howdy Doody.

....

JOHN W. HINCKLEY, JR., WENT

to court in 1989 seeking permission to communicate with the press so that he could refute the "image of me as this sick, depressed psychotic person." A psychiatrist arguing that Hinckley was still not well presented letters Hinckley had written during the previous two years in which he referred to Charles Manson as a "prophet" and a "cool dude." In another, he asked his correspondent, "Why not draw a picture of Jodie Foster for me in the nude?"

....

WHEN IN ROME
• •

ACCORDING TO A 1989 INTER-
view, the villagers of Turalei, Sudan, have no idea of
just how successful former villager (and now professional basketball player) Manute Bol has become. "If
Manute is still alive, tell him his wife has married
another man and most of his cattle were stolen ..."
said his uncle. "If he has no cows, and he wants to
marry an American wife, we can get the cows together for him," said the deputy chief of the village.
"Just let us know how many cows the woman's family
demands."

• •

THE INDIAN GOVERNMENT WAS
forced to release thousands of scavenger turtles into
the Ganges River to clean up pollution caused by
thousands of decomposing bodies thrown into it annu-

ally. Whole corpses, along with partially cremated bodies, are traditionally thrown into the river by Hindus who believe the water to have holy properties.

....

TWO WOMEN GIVING BIRTH IN

the Philippine village of Lutayan during a firefight between government troops and Muslim rebels named their baby boys after weapons used in the fighting— Bazooka and Armalite.

....

RELATIONS WORSENED BE-

tween white civil servants in Brazil's Community Affairs Department and some natives from the Fulni-O Indian tribe, working for another government office, when both were forced by budget cutbacks to use the same staff bus. The Fulni-Os are the only known Brazilian tribe that accepts openly homosexual relations, recognizes marriages between two men, and has no social taboos on heterosexual conduct, with partners ignoring age, family, or other limits. They are so free of inhibitions that sexual relations between men of the tribe can be indulged in at any place or time. The white civil servants complained to police of "physical assaults" by the Fulni-Os while the Fulni-Os lodged complaints of discrimination.

....

INDONESIAN FOREIGN MINISTER

Mochtar Kusumaatmadja told University students that

Indonesians waste too much time chatting, holding parties, and sitting on the toilet. "If you go to the toilet, do not sit there too long. That is not necessary. That kind of attitude is not what Indonesia wants."

....

SAEED AL-SAYYAF, WHOSE

name means "happy swordsman executioner," beheaded more than six hundred criminals as the official executioner of Saudi Arabia. On the job for more than thirty-five years, Al-Sayyaf's starting salary was $36 a month plus an additional $133 "for each head." "I always look forward to the opportunity to chop off more heads so that I can earn more money," he said. Al-Sayyaf's most memorable execution was twelve beheadings in one session in 1979.

....

WHEN IN IRAQ . . .

Hundreds of poets attending the Mirbad Poetry Festival in Iraq in 1987 were transported to the front lines of the Iraq-Iran war, where some read verse to Iraqi artillery teams while they were shelling the enemy. . . . Iraq's Revolutionary Command Council decreed in March 1990 that an Iraqi man who kills, "even with premeditation, his own mother, daughter, sister, aunt, niece or his cousin on his father's side, for adultery, will not be brought to justice." Men were also allowed to kill the lovers of their female relatives "if the act of adultery takes place in the family home."

....

RIOTS IN BANGLADESH KILLED

one and injured as many as two hundred when Muslims reacted violently in protest of a new sandal which carried a design that they said resembled the Arab script for Allah. Executives of the Canadian-based Bata Shoe Company were ordered into court to explain the design.

IT SEEMED LIKE A GOOD IDEA AT THE TIME

••••••••••••••••••••••••••••••••••

JERRY HODGE, VICE CHAIRMAN of the Texas Board of Criminal Justice, shed much light on the practice of using prison inmates to train bloodhounds when he invited friends along on the exercises and had jackets made up with "The Ultimate Hunt" embroidered on them. In the training, inmates, called "dog boys," are released on the prison grounds with a one-hour head start before the hounds are set on their trail. As many as ten dogs track one man. Several of the inmates, lacking protective clothing, have been bitten.

••••••••••••••••••••••••••••••••••••

MICHAEL MONTHEARD, TWENTY-four, of Danbury, Connecticut, panicked when a friend died in his car (apparently from asphyxiating on his own vomit). He drove to his parents' house, secretly buried the body in a shallow grave, then waited a week before telephoning his mother to tell her what he had done.

···

A BORED SOVIET HUNTER BEGAN

firing his gun at power lines and ended up blacking out a city of 140,000 people, resulting in an estimated loss of $1.5 million in industrial production.

···

J. MICHAEL DICKERSON, TWENTY-

eight, of Warren, Ohio, lost a $50 bet when he only managed to drink eighteen of thirty shots of cognac before he collapsed and choked to death.

···

AS A GIMMICK, PAUL WRENN, A

small, stocky Baptist minister in Christopher, Illinois, allows worshipers to jump onto his stomach, drives nails into boards with his hands, and lifts worshipers by his teeth using a special mouthpiece attached to a leather strap. During a 1988 demonstration, he lifted a 385-pound coal miner five inches off the ground before the mouthpiece slipped, leaving five of Wrenn's teeth dangling from his mouth. He calmly finished the sermon and then requested medical attention, which necessitated eight shots of a painkiller before the roots could be extracted.

···

EIGHTEEN-YEAR-OLD RONALD

Kramer of East Wenatchee, Washington, was arrested along with three friends after they got drunk, dug up a body in a cemetery, and took it to the home of a friend in the middle of the night as a joke. The body was at least seventy years old.

....

POSTAL CARRIER JOHN CADE

was placed on five years' probation for having hoarded three tons of undelivered mail in his home, much of it buried in the backyard, for three years. Cade said he started hiding leftover mail at home so his superiors wouldn't think he was inadequate at the job, then saw things start to get out of hand.

....

TONY T. COWARD AND TWO

other men pled guilty to using dynamite to fish for bass in Virginia's Smith Mountain Lake in 1989.

....

GOVERNMENT INVESTIGATORS

examined reports that Captain Cesar Garcez, thirty-two, flew his Boeing 737 off course for three hours before crash landing in the Brazilian jungle because he was listening to a football match on the radio.

....

MARK MOELLER, EIGHTEEN, AND

a friend allegedly broke into Chicago's Bohemian National Cemetery and attempted to open the grave of former Chicago Mayor Anton Cermak, who was assassinated in 1933. Police said that they wanted to pose with his body in a photograph.

....

TWO ESCAPED CONVICTS, IAN
Oppenshaw, twenty-two, and John Corbett, forty, were arrested hours after their escape from England's Dartmoor Prison at a house less than a mile away. They had stopped for afternoon tea.

....

GRENADE-WIELDING ZHANG
Yongsheng died during his attempted robbery of a bank in China's Henan province when a cashier and another customer threw the grenades back at him. Yongsheng was holding seven sticks of dynamite at the time.

....

THE STAFF AT STOCKHOLM'S
Skansen Park Zoo killed and ate Molly, a two-year-old bear cub, because overcrowding forced them to cut back on the number of cubs. "Molly was so nice, I didn't take a bite," said one.

....

SIX BALTIMORE FIREFIGHTERS
defied a forty-year tradition of washing firetrucks by

hand and instead took Aerial Tower 122, a forty-five-foot-long, high-tech vehicle, capable of extending ladders one hundred feet into the air, through the washing system used for city buses. The truck got stuck halfway through and the cleaning brushes did $10,000 worth of damage as they tore off hydraulic lines, knocked off equipment, and damaged the basket used to lift firefighters.

· ·

KEVIN FORD AND DONALD MCNAIR

were charged with various driving-related offenses in Buffalo, New York, after Ford's brother, Montgomery, drove Kevin's car up a telephone pole guide wire, causing the car to flip over. Kevin explained that he had been drinking and turned the keys over to Montgomery, who is blind, but who "always wanted to drive."

· ·

THE GREAT PRETENDERS

· ·

RICHARD L. BURNITT POSED AS

a federal agent when he convinced proprietors of a liquor store in Warsaw, New York, that he needed to take over their store for an undercover operation. Burnitt took advantage of them for seven months, using their car, drinking their liquor, and threatening to harm them if they interfered.

· ·

FOR TWO YEARS DUKE UNIVER-

sity student Mauro Cortez, Jr., thirty-seven, passed himself off to school officials and fellow students as Baron Maurice Jeffrey Locke de Rothschild, son of the wealthy French industrialist Guy de Rothschild. Cortez, who was actually from El Paso, managed to explain away various lapses in his story, including his poor grades in a beginning French course and the fact that he drove a Honda CRX instead of a more expensive car. He was eventually indicted for embezzling $1,200 from a fund he set up to raise money for cancer victims.

....

MICHAEL W. TAYLOR, TWENTY-

eight, of Louisville, Kentucky, posed as seventeen-year-old Prince Sparkle of Morocco at Meadowdale High School in Dayton, Ohio, for more than two months.

....

A MAN DRESSED IN A TOLL-

taker's uniform stood in a booth at Tampa, Florida's Crosstown Expressway one day and collected money from motorists for several hours before being detected.

....

AUTHORITIES FOUND OUT THAT

Fyodor Kuznetsov, thirty, was not a real doctor when someone tried to write up the biography of the popular Leningrad general practitioner. Kuznetsov was so well liked for his prescriptions of tea, honey, and "very generous" sick leave that patients praised him in letters to *Pravda* and requested that his portrait be hung at the Health Ministry. Kuznetsov had held jobs as a piano tuner, salesman, and cloakroom attendant before forging his medical papers.

....

DARRELL BROWN, FIFTY-THREE,

was convicted of defrauding the Veterans Administration of more than $700,000 by feigning paralysis for more than twenty years. He had been faithfully reporting to VA facilities during that time in a wheelchair after having bound his arms and legs tightly for days before visits so they would temporarily atrophy.

PAMELA JONES OF LEXINGTON,

Kentucky, thought she was marrying San Francisco 49ers quarterback Joe Montana in a 1986 ceremony, but a suspicious minister determined that the groom was an impostor. "But he told me he was Joe, and he had the NFL jacket," Jones reportedly told the minister. John Ford, thirty-nine, was in fact already married to another woman who believed him to be Hank Williams, Jr., and he was charged with swindling $10,000 from a third fiancée.

KIDS

AN EIGHTH-GRADE PHOENIX GIRL
held her English class hostage for an hour with a .357
Magnum because she was upset that her girlfriends
wouldn't talk to her.

A TEN-YEAR-OLD BOY IN KNOX-
ville, Tennessee, took over $3,000 of his father's money
and began passing out $5, $10, $20, and $100 bills to his
fourth-grade classmates in an attempt to buy their
friendship.

A LOW-FLYING PLANE CAUGHT
eight-year old DeAndra Anrig's kite, lifted her ten

feet above the ground, and dragged her two hundred feet across a park in Palo Alto, California.

....

A GROUP OF BALTIMORE TEEN-

agers held a contest during the annual March of Dimes walkathon in which the one who landed the best punch on one of the charity walkers would receive a cardboard replica of a prizefighter's championship belt. The group was linked to eleven attacks on walkers.

....

A GROUP OF FIVE BOYS IN IN-

dian Harbour Beach, Florida, spent four days rescuing a kitten from a drainage pipe, finally capturing it by lowering fish tied onto a badminton net. The boys named the kitten Baby Jessica Too.

....

ANTWAN ROBINSON, EIGHTEEN,

and his sixteen-year-old brother were charged in Miami with kidnaping after abducting an eighteen-year-old woman at 8:30 one evening. By 9:30, they realized they had taken the wrong woman and that the ransom would not be paid. Robinson then abandoned the plan because he had to be home by 10:00 or he would set off the alarm on his ankle beeper, which he wore as a condition of his release from jail for another crime.

....

A GROUP OF BOYS PLAYED A

game of soccer on a South Bronx street with a human head wrapped in rags before the father of one of the boys realized what their "ball" really was. They had found it in a box of trash. Police found dismembered arms and legs nearby but no torso.

AFTER HIS MOTHER REFUSED TO

give him a Coke, a six-year-old boy in Lille, France, took a hunting rifle from a closet, loaded it, and shot her in the abdomen.

AN ELEVEN-YEAR-OLD BOY IN

Manila wrote a note to his sixth-grade science teacher threatening her life unless she gave grades of 90 to 95 to the boy and ten of his friends. Warning "Don't play with your life," the boy signed the letter "Mr. Killer." The teacher noted that the boy was to have received a grade of 88.

FIREFIGHTERS IN SAN JOSE,

California, had to chisel three-year-old Jennifer Camilleri's foot free from the toilet. Jennifer had been standing on the toilet to wash a toy pony in the sink when she slipped and got stuck. Two years earlier Jennifer was almost strangled when her sweater caught on a fence after she climbed a wood pile to reach over a fence and pet a neighbor's dog.

....

SEVEN-YEAR-OLD JASON RICHE

drove himself to school in a 1980 Buick belonging to his mother's boyfriend after complaining that it was raining outside. Minutes after telling him to go back outside and wait for the bus, Jason's mother saw him driving away. Jason drove the five-kilometer distance to his Ontario school without incident.

....

STATEN ISLAND FAMILY COURT

Judge Daniel D. Leddy, Jr., barred a sixteen-year-old boy and his thirteen-year-old brother from watching professional wrestling on television because they injured each other in reenactments of the matches, performing body slams, choke holds, and figure-four leg locks. The thirteen-year-old would assume the persona of "Rowdy" Roddy Piper, threatening his mother with "the terrible things he was going to do to her." He once put a "sleep hold" on her while she was cooking at the stove.

ACCIDENTS
WILL HAPPEN
· ·

THE TUSCOLA HIGH SCHOOL
marching band in Waynesville, North Carolina, practicing on the school's parking lot, froze in their steps as an Oldsmobile Cierra driven by seventeen-year-old classmate Sean Sojack drove through their formation. Sojack's father said that his son, new to driving to school, simply saw an opening in the ranks and went for it.

· ·

JAMES A. VANDERMEER,
twenty-five, was charged with driving while intoxicated after Rochester police found the body of Gilbert T. Nettles, Jr., twenty-six, caught in the windshield of Vandermeer's car. Police estimate that Nettles was carried nine miles on the hood from the site where he was struck.

In a similar accident in Lantana, Florida, one year earlier, seventy-four-year-old Stanley Dobek allegedly drove for four miles with the body of bicyclist John Davis, forty-two, sticking through his windshield and into the passenger seat of his car.

....

PRAVDA REPORTED IN AUGUST

1989 that one of two maintenance workers investigating a gas leak in the basement of an apartment house in the Ukraine struck a match and set off an explosion killing eighteen people. V. Marushchak, the worker who struck the match, was killed, but his partner survived.

....

A ONE-VEHICLE COLLISION

created thirty-four casualties near the town of Pantar in the Philippines. A Coca-Cola delivery truck lost its brakes and overturned, killing seven of the thirty-four hitchhikers on board and wounding the other twenty-seven.

....

AN ALASKAN AIRLINES BOEING

737 was struck by a fish on takeoff from the Juneau, Alaska, airport in March 1987, causing a delay during which the plane was inspected for damage. The fish had been dropped by a bald eagle.

....

NEW JERSEY STATE POLICE SAY

that a man may have been hit by as many as twenty-one cars on the Garden State Parkway on the night of September 24, 1990. A man who pulled off the road to help "continually heard thumps that he believed to be the body being hit again and again," said police.

CHEF ALBERT GRABHAM OF THE

New House Hotel in Wales hid the restaurant's New Year's Eve earnings in the oven. He failed to remember that when he lit the same oven to prepare New Year's Day lunch.

DENISE WILLIAMS, TWENTY-

seven, was thrown fifty feet from a car in which she was a passenger when it was struck from behind by a car driven by her boyfriend. She crashed through the roof of Syble Cherry's house and landed feet first on the refrigerator. "She got up, walked into my living room, and lay down on my couch," said Cherry. "I guess anything is possible." The car Williams was in was the second car to crash into Cherry's house in less than a year.

TACOMA POLICE OFFICER KERRY

Filbert stopped a car after he witnessed a basset hound alongside it being dragged by a leash stuck in the car's door. Filbert said the dog was "picking them up and putting them down just about as fast as he could." He estimated that the dog reached twenty to twenty-five miles per hour and "rolled several times" before he could stop the car. The man and woman in the car said that they had shut the door on his leash so that he wouldn't wander and then forgot about him. The dog, eight-month-old Tattoo, seemed unharmed.

··

SIX GUNMEN ARMED WITH A

shotgun, an automatic rifle, and handguns opened fire on the Bridgeport, Connecticut, home of DeLen McRae, forty-four, an associate Baptist minister. The gunfire broke windows, pierced walls and furniture, and even struck McRae's clerical robe where it hung. Hours later the gunmen called McRae to apologize because they had fired on his house by mistake, thinking that a neighbor lived there because his car was parked in front.

··

ACCORDING TO WITNESSES ON

the ground, the pilots of two small planes flying near Denali National Park in Alaska were so preoccupied with watching a moose that they crashed into each other.

··

NINETEEN PEOPLE ICE-FISHING

on Minnesota's Lake Mille Lacs had to be rescued

from a large ice floe after the ice broke free and carried them more than half a mile out into the lake. The ice-fishers, rescued by boat, left behind ten ice-houses and three all-terrain vehicles on the floe.

....

BRIAN PETERSON, THIRTY-FIVE,

of New Britain, Connecticut, died after a woman sat on his lap while he was seated on top of a glass table. The glass cracked, with one piece nearly severing one of his arms.

....

BUS TALES

....

DARIUS McCOLLUM, TWENTY-
five, of Queens, admitted stealing thirteen buses from
Transit Authority depots in one year. Described by
New York police as a "bus buff," McCollum was wearing an actual bus driver's uniform when he was
caught.

....

THE TRACK TEAM FROM HEN-
ninger High School in Syracuse, New York, was left
stranded after their bus driver dropped them off in
the rain to inspect a tournament playing field in the
Bronx while he was to have searched for a parking
space. New York police found an empty bus early the
next morning.

....

DIANE MONTIERO, A GREY-

hound bus passenger, took over the wheel for a trip from Delaware to New York after the replacement driver admitted that he didn't know how to drive a manual transmission.

....

OUTRAGED WHEN *THE MESA*

(Arizona) *Tribune* printed a color photo of Mark Tracy, twenty-five, after he had been electrocuted, a friend apparently retaliated by ramming the newspaper building's lobby with a bus on which he had painted "thanks for nothing."

....

LOCK
YOUR DOORS

• •

A SOUTH BRONX STREET GANG

called The Powerules requires that new members shoot someone in the leg as an initiation rite. The gang's emblem is the cross hairs of a telescopic sight.

• •

THE SECRET SERVICE ARRESTED

Christopher E. Jackson, thirty-three, after he allegedly slit the throat of a live duck and impaled it on a spike of the White House fence.

• •

POLICE IN WASHINGTON STATE

labeled Christian Agar's death "suspicious" when the twenty-five-year-old Seattle man's body was found completely wrapped in duct tape near U.S. Highway 101.

His body was detected after the "mummy shaped object" was X-rayed.

....

JAMES D. CURTRIGHT, TWENTY-
one, a deaf mute, pleaded innocent by reason of insanity to charges of killing his mother and sister. Curtright used sign language to tell the jury that his sister had an abortion after his mother coerced her into having sex with a man in exchange for a microwave oven. He then said that he had a long talk with someone who claimed to be God before he stabbed both women to death.

....

A MILWAUKEE JURY FOUND
twenty-seven-year old Deborah Kazuck guilty of the attempted ax murder of Jeffrey Meka as part of a ritual which Kazuck believed would bring Jack the Ripper back from the dead. She reportedly believed that Jack the Ripper was her son in a previous life. Meka was lured to Kazuck's apartment by two other women and was attacked by Kazuck when he used the bathroom. She sprang from behind a shower curtain chanting "redrum" and hit Meka in the head with a hatchet. Her plan was to dismember him, drain his blood, and eat his kidneys.

....

AS PORTLAND, OREGON, POLICE
tried for forty minutes to talk down a transient threat-

ening to jump from a bridge above the Willamette River, at least one among dozens of boaters in the water below yelled "Jump!" Scores of onlookers at the nearby Rose Festival Fun Center then cheered as the man finally jumped or fell into the river.

···

BALTIMORE POLICE CHARGED

thirty-year-old Clifton Earl Williams with murdering his mother after he allegedly attacked her with a circular saw while she slept. Police say that Williams connected several extension cords together to reach her bedroom with the saw.

···

POLICE IN PLATTSBURGH, NEW

York, were baffled by a number of cases in which a man pretending to be a doctor telephoned children and tried to persuade them to strangle their siblings. He told one eleven-year-old, "If you don't want your little brother to die, you must strangle him immediately."

···

ACCORDING TO WITNESSES, A

man drove up to the Otto (North Carolina) Texaco and Food Mart one night in a pickup truck and began showing off a dead four-foot rattlesnake. Another man, apparently intoxicated, took the snake and began petting and kissing its mouth. Then he opened the snake's mouth and began slapping his hand with it until he began to bleed, at which point he jumped into a truck and drove away.

....

A MAN DUBBED "THE BURPER"

hassled police in Lincoln, Pennsylvania, by breaking into their radio calls to play Christmas carols by blowing on a kazoo, whistling, and belching.

....

TESTIFYING AT MICHAEL D.

Proctor's murder trial, psychiatrist Richard S. Epstein said that Proctor was a case of multiple personalities and that he knew of at least six of them. Epstein said there was "Clarence," a satanist; "Tufu," a demonlike Pekingese dog who demanded blood sacrifice; "Abdul," a Muslim; "Vic," a man who enjoyed cooking; "Rick," a teenager who loved racing cars; and "Thriller," who appeared when Proctor pledged a college fraternity.

....

A MAN IN HIS TWENTIES FROM

Tasmania jumped into the ape enclosure at the Melbourne Zoo screaming "I've come to kill a gorilla!" He then kicked and punched a 220-pound primate before zoo officials locked him in a cage.

....

666 NEWS

• •

THE BRITISH DRIVING, VEHICLE

and Licensing Center announced in early 1990 that they were dropping the numbers 666 from car license plates after the holders of such plates complained that their cars and/or their lives were cursed with all sorts of problems because of them. One man complained that within the first week of receiving his 666 plate his house had been burglarized, his water supply was poisoned, and a truck backed over his car.

A similar incident occurred in Tennessee in 1988 when the state issued new three-digit plates. Davidson County withdrew more than 300 plates bearing 666 from the county allotment after drivers refused to accept them.

• •

ONE HUNDRED SENIOR CITIZENS

at a Gary, Indiana, apartment complex petitioned the

city housing authority to change their street address from 666 Jackson Street because it was the sign of the Antichrist. The president of the apartment's tenant council said that "some religious people . . . moved out."

....

DURING 1980 AND 1981 THE IN-
ternal Revenue Service asked taxpayers to enter the number 666 as a code on a form reporting individual retirement accounts. The IRS said that the Social Security Administration chose the number because a scanner could read it easily. After complaints from fundamentalist Christians, the IRS changed the number on 1982 forms to 555.

....

SECRET SERVICE AGENTS AP-
prehended Gregory Stuart Gordon, thirty-two, of Los Angeles, after he scaled the fence of former President Ronald Reagan's house in Bel-Air, California. A man calling himself Gordon telephoned the Associated Press to say that he believed Reagan to be the Antichrist "and I'm the second coming of Christ." The Reagan's home address had been changed from 666 St. Cloud Drive to 668.

....

WHAT'S IN A NAME?

• •

THE NAZI BAR IN BANGKOK,

Thailand, adorned with photos of Nazi storm troopers and caricatures of Hitler, changed its name in 1988 after complaints by foreigners. "We don't want to offend even a few people, so we're experimenting with a new, neutral name and decor," said manager Aor Sarayuk of the renamed "No Name" bar.

....

CALIFORNIAN ENRIQUE SILBERG

changed his name in 1985 to Ubiquitous Perpetuity God after a judge refused to allow him to change it to simply "God."

....

ANTHONY MBA, A NIGERIAN,

filed a $1.1-million harassment suit against a Brooks

Brothers store in the Westfarms Mall in West Hartford, Connecticut, after a clerk refused to honor his American Express Gold card, saying, "Come on, that's not your name, that's a degree."

···

AFTER ADDING ANOTHER "Z" TO

his name, Zeke Zzzyzus (formerly Zzyzus) retained his place as the last name in the Montreal telephone directory. Zzzyzus beat Zzyzyx, Pol Zzyzzo, and Zzzap Distribution for last place.

···

LELAND ROGER BRUNS WENT TO

Hennepin County (Minnesota) District Court to formally change his name to Modern Man. Noting that he had been fascinated with "modern man" since his youth, Man said, "I never felt I was the person I was told to be. I feel good now."

···

COLLECTORS

· ·

WHEN QUESTIONED BY POLICE,
John Roeleveld, seventy-two, said that God had instructed him to put together his collection of 250,000 stuffed animals and birds in preparation for the end of the world. He said that God told him to collect two of every species and promised to raise the whole collection from the dead. Police found the menagerie buried in concrete bomb shelters Roeleveld had built around his house in the Netherlands village of Eerbeek. The collection included crocodiles, ostriches, kangaroos, panthers, apes, a bear, an elephant skull, and a camel.

· ·

BOB ENGEL, A NATIONAL LEAGUE
umpire, was charged with stealing 4,180 baseball cards from a store in Bakersfield, California. Asked by po-

lice why he took the cards, Engel reportedly said, "To collect and trade."

···

STEPHEN C. BLUMBERG, FORTY-

one, was arrested by the FBI in connection with the theft of a number of rare books and manuscripts. Agents found his home in Ottumwa, Iowa, crammed with perhaps as many as 11,000 rare books worth at least an estimated $20 million. Books found there belonging to the University of Oregon's special collection of historical documents were alone worth $662,000. It took seven trips with a moving van to remove evidence from the house. Blumberg is also considered a leading collector of brass doorknobs and stained-glass windows, along with other antiques. He traveled the country is search of antiques and had warehouses full of objects in several cities. "This son of mine is an oddball if you ever saw one," said his father. "I myself call him eccentric," said his mother.

···

LOTTO FEVER

· ·

RETIRED BRIGADIER GENERAL
Alfredo Lim, Director of the National Bureau of Investigation, was assigned by President Corazón Aquino to investigate charges of fixing at the Philippines state lottery's September 1, 1990, drawing. At the September 16 drawing, which was specially televised in hopes of restoring public confidence in the game, Lim stepped forward with the winning ticket to collect the $200,000 top prize.

· ·

ROBERT KEMPTON, TWENTY, OF
Pompano Beach, Florida, told police that he faked three robberies at the store where he worked in order to steal $4,000 to feed his lottery addiction of fifty tickets a day.

· ·

WILLIAM CURRY, THIRTY-

seven, of Boston, died of a heart attack two weeks after winning $3.6 million in the Massachusetts Megabucks lottery. "It was the stress of it that killed him," said a relative. Curry was reportedly hounded by accountants, financial advisors, and requests for cash in the days after his win.

THE NEW YORK STATE LOTTERY

had to suspend play on the number 3569 before noon on December 27, 1989, because it had been played by too many people. This was the number of the license plate (VR3569) on the truck New York Yankees manager Billy Martin was killed in days earlier.

WINNERS OF A LOTTERY IN THE

Ukrainian city of Stakhanov often walk away with rolls of toilet paper, towels, pigs, hens, goats, detergent, and bath soap as their prizes. "But don't forget that there are great shortages," said the newspaper *Literary Gazette*. "In the city of Stakhanov, except for the lottery, one cannot get these goods." Tickets cost 50 kopeks (about 81 cents), which is more than the cost of many prizes.

WHILE TACOMA, WASHINGTON,

police prepared to tranquilize a black bear running

laps around the city's reservoir, a bookie stood by taking bets on the bear's time.

....

AN ERROR BY AN ARIZONA

court resulted in Bonita Lynch becoming one-fourth owner of her ex-husband's $2.2 million lottery jackpot. A paperwork error delayed their official divorce date for eleven days, and it was during that time that Mr. Lynch won the lottery.

....

JUMPED
THE GUN

• •

A SEVENTEEN-YEAR-OLD PINE tree in the Chinese village of Xinfu, which attracted forty thousand people with stories of the miraculous healing power of the water raining down from its leaves, was found actually to be dripping with the urine of millions of insects.

• •

ENGLISH PHYSICIST ANTHONY B. Wooldridge went public in 1987 with two photographs taken on a Himalayan mountain trail which he termed the "best-yet evidence" for the existence of the yeti, the legendary creature often referred to as the "Abominable Snowman." Upon further analysis he conceded months later that the object in the photos was "in reality, a rock."

• •

SOON AFTER PRONOUNCING A

tenant dead, New York City medical investigator Jules Lisner proceeded to notify the building management company and asked if he could put down a deposit on the $300-a-month rent-controlled apartment. "It was bad judgment," said Lisner after being officially reprimanded.

....

GERMANY'S RED ARMY FACTION

terrorist group sent a letter to the Federal Prosecutor's Office taking responsibility for the assassination of Agriculture Minister Ignaz Kiechle at his sixtieth birthday party on March 3. The letter was dated March 2. The next day the Red Army sent another letter saying that the operation had been aborted and that due to a "mistake in coordination" the letter was sent before the assassination took place.

....

CHARLES BODECK, SEVENTY-

three, shot his sixty-seven-year-old wife to death and then killed himself with a 12-gauge shotgun, apparently motivated by an obsessive fear of Lyme disease, which is most commonly transmitted by deer tick bites. Bodeck had twice been to doctors who told him that he had not contracted the disease from tick bites he had received over years of fur-trapping and that he had not passed it to his wife. Police found the Bodecks' mailbox filled with information on the disease and discovered that he had scheduled yet another appointment to have a Lyme-disease test done.

....

UGANDA WAS RIFE WITH COUP

rumors after a newsman on the state-run radio was heard to say "Oh my God!" over the air, followed shortly by "Good night" and the station going off the air. He was actually reacting to the sight of a poisonous snake slithering into the radio studio.

....

ASTROPHYSICIST JOHN MIDDLE-

ditch told a 1990 American Association for the Advancement of Science audience that a signal thought the previous year to be the fastest-spinning object in the universe—and thus the subject of many theories and papers that dominated meetings the previous twelve months—was in fact just reception from a TV monitor in the Chilean observatory where the "spinning object" had been discovered. Someone had forgotten to turn the monitor off.

....

PUT SOME CLOTHES ON

· ·

SIXTY MEMBERS OF THE Corsican National Liberation Front invaded a nudist camp near Bastia, holding about fifty vacationing nudists at gunpoint as they blew up sixty cabins.

· ·

DURING HIS CAMPAIGN FOR CIR- cuit court judge in Sioux Falls, South Dakota, Richard Hopewell, fifty-three, admitted to a 1978 incident in which he appeared nude in a local drug store but claimed that he was under the influence of PCP at the time, administered by "a secret agent of a political adversary."

· ·

GASLIGHTS RECORDS IN MEL- bourne, Australia, holds an annual "Nude Day" dur-

BEYOND NEWS OF THE WEIRD

ing which each nude patron gets a free record. Seventy records were given away during the 1990 observance.

....

THE 1988 NATIONAL NUDE WEEK-

end at the Hidden Valley Nudist Resort near Dawsonville, Georgia, saw eight nude male skydivers jump out of a plane at 3,500 feet and land in a field.

....

BEN MASEL'S CAMPAIGN POST-

ers for the Illinois Republican gubernatorial primary featured Masel nude with the slogan "Nothing to Hide."

....

VIRGINIA GENERAL DISTRICT

Court Judge G. Blair Harry dismissed an indecent exposure charge filed against Robert V. Gallup, thirty-seven, after an anonymous caller complained that he was riding his lawn mower in the nude. "It is not something I certainly advocate," said the judge. "But who am I to judge how a person is to cut his grass?" Gallup had been charged two years earlier with washing his car in the nude.

....

MARYLAND STATE POLICE WERE

on the lookout for a man wearing a disposable diaper and a T-shirt and reportedly driving a sports car with

a backseat filled with cans of whipped cream after reports that he had been seen crossing over the state line from Pennsylvania. It was his third reported excursion into Maryland that year.

....

I CALL IT ART

. . . .

ARTIST RICK GIBSON HAD TO

flee an angry crowd after animal rights activists foiled his plan to crush Sniffy the rat with a fifty-five-pound concrete block between two artists' canvases. Gibson is known for other avant-garde art productions, including trying to eat part of a human testicle and making earrings from human fetuses.

. . . .

FRENCH ARTIST CHANTAL COT-

tet invented what she calls "blast art"—sculpting steel with the use of dynamite, hand grenades, and artillery shells. While she can handle the dynamite and hand grenades by herself, she takes advantage of planned artillery or missile fire at nearby military bases by positioning her raw steel material at the target sites.

. . . .

THE LOS ANGELES CITY ATTOR-

ney accused Daniel Ramos, eighteen, of painting the word "Chaka" on ten thousand sites in Southern California, from utility poles to buildings, walls, and traffic signs, causing an estimated $500,000 in damages.

....

NICK ALTAMURO, WHILE A STU-

dent at the Pennsylvania Academy of Fine Arts, said that his intention was to "bash the public's head up against reality." Among his works were an array of twenty rats' heads, which had to be removed from an exhibit because of the smell, and a dead cat in a container filled with antifreeze, which exploded in a gallery after the cat absorbed the antifreeze.

....

GERMAN ARTIST JOSEPH BEUYS,

an experimenter in the use of fat as an art material, once went so far as to re-create a corner of a pedestrian underpass near Münster University out of twenty tons of mutton fat. The model is now displayed at the Guggenheim in New York City.

....

MARC ADAMS, A SENIOR FINE

arts student at San Jose State University, was detained by police for indecent exposure after donning a homemade clear vinyl suit and mask over his nude body and lying down on a table in front of the university's art building. Adams entitled his work *Kinetic Composition on a Cube.*

● ●

THE BEGINNING OF THE END

· ·

LATE IN JULY OF 1989 A KITTEN with eight legs and two tails was born in the village of Machala in Ecuador. Rejected by its mother, it died within hours. The devout Catholic population there saw it as a bad sign. "We are nearing the end of the world because people are so decadent," said one.

· ·

IN JUNE OF 1990 A LARGE group of King Penguins stampeded at Macquarie Island's Lusitania Bay near Tasmania, leaving seven thousand dead. The estimated six thousand chicks and one thousand adults were stacked four deep, with wildlife officials describing the scene as something akin to a sports stadium crowd. Officials were dumbfounded as to the cause.

· ·

MEXICAN POLICE CHARGED

three police officers with the hanging of 150 horses outside the town of Tecpan de Galeano over a three-month period. The three belong to a satanic cult named The Green Scorpion. The horses had been strangled, had their throats cut, and were found hanging from trees by ropes.

....

IN AUGUST 1990 HUNDREDS OF

Burmese citizens flocked to shrines where the images of Buddha were reportedly weeping, bleeding, or changing shape. The news was viewed as a bad omen for that country's political future.

....

A PORTRAIT OF SAINT IRENE,

the patron saint of peace and the sick, drew thousands to the Saint Irene Chrysovalantou Cathedral, a Greek Orthodox church in Queens, with reports that the icon was crying over the Persian Gulf conflict. The icon reportedly began crying on October 17, 1990, following a service dedicated to peace in the Middle East while it was on loan to a sister church in Chicago. When it was brought back to Queens, word of the crying brought thousands to the church.

....

AMAZONINO MENDES, GOVER-

nor of Brazil's Amazonas State, announced that he

was fulfilling a campaign promise when he offered to distribute free power saws to settlers in the Amazon rain forest region. The saws reportedly cut down trees ten times faster than axes.

....

POLITICS 101

DURING HER CAMPAIGN FOR A
seat in the Taiwanese legislature, thirty-year-old model Hsu Hsiao-dan bared her breasts several times in demonstrations demanding more democracy. Once while posing as the Goddess of Democracy on the steps outside the legislature. Said Hsu, "My body is a political weapon. My breasts are nuclear warheads."

TEXAS CONGRESSIONAL CANDI-
date Steve "Bo" Sawyer handed out bullets while he campaigned, telling potential voters, "If I don't shoot straight, shoot me." Said Sawyer later, "I think it scared a few people when I gave it to them. I handed one to a girl on the University of Texas campus, and she just looked scared of me. It made me feel bad."

1990 NEW YORK REPUBLICAN

gubernatorial candidate Pierre Rinfret had difficulty establishing voter name recognition. A *New York Times* reporter's informal survey of voters identified Pierre Rinfret as an artist, a perfume, a drug dealer, a movie star, a fashion designer, a chef, the French ambassador to the United States, and a goalie for the New York Rangers.

....

OKLAHOMA DISTRICT JUDGE

candidate Josh J. Evans lost 91 percent of the vote to Frank Ogden, the incumbent, who died months before election day but whose name remained on the ballot. People opposed to Evans actually campaigned for the dead Ogden, theorizing that his victory would result in the seat being declared vacant and a gubernatorial appointment to fill it. The bar association of Craig County even endorsed Ogden.

....

THERE'S A MACHINE IN MY HEAD

· ·

ACCORDING TO A 1985 GALLUP

Poll, about 16 million Americans have experienced hearing inner voices or auditory hallucinations. Other surveys have shown that 10 percent of the population has heard voices.

· ·

AFTER HAVING BEEN ARRESTED

for shoplifting at least once a month from May 1979 through May 1983, and having been convicted thirty-seven times, LePonds Shaffer, thirty, told a Chicago courtroom that doctors had implanted a radio transmitter in his neck by which they distorted his ability to distinguish right from wrong.

· ·

NEIGHBORS SAY THAT DANIEL

Patrick Lynam of Federal Way, Washington, who killed seven members of his family and then himself, had been obsessed with the idea that someone was making embarrassing films of his life. He also reportedly received messages from radio and television shows, even going so far as to take notes on the *Today* show each morning, recording what he thought were messages about him.

....

JERRY LEE DUNBAR PLED

guilty to the strangling of a woman in an Alexandria, Virginia, motel. He hid her body under the floor of the motel room. In a pretrial conversation with a psychiatrist, Dunbar said that he is often surrounded by little people who glow in the dark and that he hears voices which give him violent instructions.

....

WITNESSES SAY THAT JAMES

Calvin Brady, thirty-one, was smiling when he opened fire in an Atlanta mall, killing one and wounding four in the spring of 1990. During questioning he told police that there was a "mechanical device" inside him controlling his actions.

....

THE USEFULNESS OF FRANKIE

Tighe, twenty, as a defense witness in the 1990 Bensonhurst murder trial was thrown into question

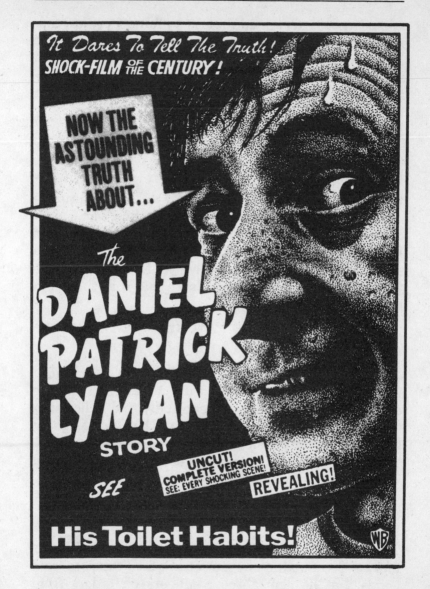

when it was determined that he suffered from hallucinations and was released from a mental hospital just two days before the murder. Asked on the witness stand if he ever told people that he was controlled by helicopters and submarines, Tighe replied, "No! Just helicopters."

···

WHEN JIMMIE PETTIT, FORTY-
three, entered Miami's Channel 4 television studios claiming that he had a bomb, the building was evacuated. Upon further inquiry it was understood that Pettit claimed that the CIA had surgically implanted a bomb in his brain twenty-five years earlier and he was only asking for help. He later said that the bomb had moved to his rectum.

···

JOHN NORTH WRIGHT OF LANS-
ing, Michigan, was charged with threatening the life of President Bush after he reportedly told police that the CIA was blackmailing him and that he was going to kill those responsible. Using the pseudonym "Dr. Kabbalah," Wright wrote books detailing what he said were attempts by the CIA to control his mind.

···

IN 1985 KWOK HOM, FIFTY-
four, of 666 Sacramento Street in San Francisco, told police that he shot three neighbors on orders from John Wayne. He also confessed to hating the sound of

running water in their building's communal shower
and the smell of the neighbor's cooking. ·

....

BERNELL HEGWOOD, EIGHTEEN,

said that he killed three employees of a fast-food
restaurant in Fort Lauderdale, Florida, because he
had been taken over by the spirit of a Louisiana
murderer.

....

SINGLE-BULLET
THEORIES

• •

ON JULY 13, 1990, SIX ARMY
communications specialists classified as AWOL since
July 9 were apprehended in Gulf Breeze, Florida. One
was picked up by police during a routine traffic stop,
one at a campground, and four at the home of a
woman known as a local psychic. All six belonged to a
classified intelligence unit at an electronic eavesdrop-
ping post in West Germany. Friends of the six relayed
various reasons for their travel from Germany to Florida, including that they had been "chosen by . . . di-
vine intervention to help prepare for the end of the
world . . . about eight years from now." One said that
they were in Gulf Breeze to await the imminent ar-
rival of a spaceship on August 6 and that the landing
would be heralded by war in Lebanon and a shake-up
of the United States military. They also believed that
Christ was to return to Earth in a spaceship. A report
in *Stars and Stripes* said that the six were on their

way to "destroy the anti-Christ." After being detained at Fort Benning, Georgia, and Fort Knox, Kentucky, for about two weeks, the six were given general discharges by the Army, which also issued a statement clearing them of any espionage activity. To add to the strangeness, the *Gulf Breeze Sentinel* and other news organizations received a cryptic teletyped message on July 25, accompanied by UFO photos. The message was a threat to the Army to "Free the Gulf Breeze Six. We have the missing files, the box of 500 + photos and the plans you want back. Here is proof with close-ups cut out. Next we send the close-ups and then everything unless they are released. Answer Code AUGSBB3CM."

....

SINCE 1982, TWENTY-FIVE PRO-

fessionals of the British defense industry have died in strange circumstances. One woman's death—she drowned in eighteen inches of water with her feet and hands bound and a noose around her neck—was listed by police as a "50/50 chance" of suicide. Other deaths were caused by driving a car into the Liverpool River; suffocating in a plastic sack with nine feet of plastic wrap around the victim's face; falling off a 240-foot suspension bridge after driving there; having a rope tied around the victim's head and the other end around a tree and then accelerating in his car; the victim driving his car into a cafe; drowning in a bathtub; being electrocuted with electrodes taped to teeth fillings; and falling from a hotel room after telling friends he feared for his life.

....

MICHAEL BREEN, THIRTY-ONE,

of Washington, D.C., was arrested after punching Senator John Glenn (D-Ohio) in the face during an outdoor television interview. Breen was reportedly saying, "The earthquakes are starting, the earthquakes are starting," at the time. Breen later told police that he did it to get the attention of the Pope so that he could reveal the "Fatima Secret" and prevent a nuclear war. Breen, an engineer at an aerospace company, said that he had been getting instructions from dreams revealing future events to him since December 1988.

....

DURING HIS TRIAL FOR THE AT-

tempted assassination of Pope John Paul II, Mehmet Ali Agca claimed that he was Christ, warned that "in this generation, the days are counted," and said that his attack on the Pope was linked to the third "Fatima Secret," which he demanded be revealed.

....

THE MYSTERIOUS CROP CIRCLES

and other strange geometric shapes appearing in the farmlands of southern England (more than 1,000 since 1980, with more than 250 appearing in 1989 and at least 400 in 1990) seem to have spread in the past two years to other countries. About 1,000 circles were reported in thirty countries in 1990 including Canada, the United States, Australia, Japan, France, Italy, the Soviet Union, Sweden, and Norway. They have appeared in corn, sorghum, and wheat fields as well as in rice paddies and on snowy plains and prairies.

....

THE PAST TWO YEARS HAVE WIT-
nessed a rash of cat mutilations in California, New Jersey, Florida, and other states. Some of the cases recall the mysterious incidents of cattle mutilations in the western United States, with cat carcasses appearing surgically dismembered, disemboweled, or skinned, a lack of blood at the scene, and paws and other body parts left near the bodies. In three months in 1989, sixty-seven cats were found mutilated in Tustin, California. In three months in 1990, Lincoln County, Maine, reported the disappearance of sixty cats, which was more than one animal shelter worker said she had ever seen in thirteen years of work. During a four-week period in 1989 in Concord, California, someone shot or stabbed to death at least twenty-six cats. Most authorities argue that urban coyotes are responsible for the mutilations. Others theorize gang and/or cult activity.

....

ADELHEID STREIDEL, FORTY-
two, was arrested for the attempted assassination of West German political party leader Oskar Lafontaine following a rally. Streidel said that she stabbed him in order to get the attention of the press when she is

tried. "I wanted to give a signal. There are people factories and underground operating theaters in Europe where people from the population are remolded physically and mentally. This takes place with the approval of politicians."

....

OK, YOU EXPLAIN IT

· ·

IN THE FIRST FIVE MONTHS OF
1990, 18 young Thai workers in Singapore who had no
previous symptoms of sickness died in their sleep.
Upon investigation, doctors determined that over 200
Thai workers had died mysteriously in Singapore since
1983, with most of the deaths attributed to heart failure.
Researchers in the United States reported 117 cases of
sudden unexplained night deaths among Vietnamese,
Laotian, and Cambodian refugees. The Thai Public
Health Ministry recorded 600 similar deaths of Thai
workers in the Middle East. While some attribute the
death wave to poverty, cardiac abnormality, or job stress,
many Thais see the deaths as "lai tai" or "nightmare
deaths." Folklore says that "widow ghosts" hunt for hus-
bands to take away in the night. Many young male Thais
in Singapore began painting their fingernails red to
trick the ghosts into thinking that they were women.

· ·

AFTER BEING PLAGUED BY

dreams that her mother, who had been listed by police as a missing person for three and a half years, was "in a place where she couldn't move, either tied up or locked up," Kelly Tyburski, twenty, broke into a locked freezer in the basement of her family's home and found her mother's body. A Detroit medical examiner said that she may have been alive when placed there. Tyburski's father was charged with the murder.

TWELVE SURVIVORS OF A FISH-

ing boat accident in the southern Philippines on Christmas Eve 1989 said that their craft was overturned by "something that looked like a giant octopus." One fisherman said that the octopus grabbed the boat's pontoons and overturned it but did not attack them.

IN 1987 THE ATLANTA HOME OF

William Winston, seventy-nine, and Minnie Winston, seventy-seven, began to bleed. Police called to investigate blood splashing "like a sprinkler" from the Winston's bathroom floor could find no explanation. Steve Cartwright, an Atlanta homicide detective, said that no bodies were discovered, only "copious amounts of blood" splattered on walls and floors in at least five rooms. A police analysis confirmed that the substance was indeed human blood.

....

BURNING HOUSE UPDATE

In a situation very similar to the cases reported in our second volume, authorities could find no rational explanation for a Wharncliffe, West Virginia, house that experienced strange fires leaping from electrical sockets. Assistant Fire Chief Kendall Simpson said that the owners, the Reverend and Mrs. Gene Clemons, reported seeing "fire shooting six inches" from electrical outlets. The fire department was first called to fight isolated fires throughout the house, including one on a mattress, another on a towel, and others on a bathroom rack, spots in the carpeting, and in closets. After fire officials disconnected all power to the house, the fires continued. When the Clemons family moved their belongings to the church next door, two bulletin boards there began to smoke. Gilbert Volunteer Fire Department Chief Jerry Grimmett called it all "something you'd see in a movie."

MAKES SENSE
TO ME

· ·

PETER FRANCONERI, A FORMER

Buildings Department official in New York City, told police that he panicked when he awoke to find that his friend, twenty-nine-year-old Laurie Sue Rosenthal, had died in his apartment. That's why he dragged the body downstairs and left it on the sidewalk outside his Manhattan apartment near some trash cans.

· ·

CHARLES MANSON HAS BEEN DE-

nied parole numerous times over the years. In 1986 he told the parole panel at San Quentin Prison that he spent his time making "scorpion dolls" which had power to torment people. He also noted that if paroled, he would participate in world revolution. He didn't attend his 1979 hearing but instead sent the panel Monopoly money and the card reading "Advance to Go, Collect $200."

....

A TRANSIENT UNABLE TO LEAVE

a tip for a waitress at a Salt Lake City restaurant told her, "I'm going to go rob a bank and I'll be back." Police arrested him after he walked out of the First Interstate Bank with $1,200 and walked back across the street to leave a $2 tip.

....

SCOTT ROBERT ROSTON, THIRTY-

seven, was sentenced to life in prison for throwing his wife overboard while on their Pacific honeymoon cruise. Roston at first said that she was blown overboard by a gust of wind but then changed his story to say that Israeli intelligence agents had framed him for her murder as part of a terror campaign they were waging against him in retaliation for a book he wrote, *Nightmare in Israel.*

....

AN ARKANSAS SQUIRREL HUNT-

er waited a day to report finding a dead body in the woods because he thought that any investigation would spoil his plans for hunting the next morning.

....

FORMER POLICE CLERK JOY UN-

derwood, thirty-four, filed a worker's compensation

claim charging that handling the evidence of seven murder victims unearthed at a Sacramento boardinghouse has caused her post-traumatic stress syndrome. Underwood claims that she vomits whenever she sees news reports of the case, has violent nightmares, and can no longer eat vegetables "because they have dirt around them, like the people dug up in [the] yard—and I'm a vegetarian."

....

WHEN ACTOR COREY FELDMAN

was asked for an explanation after being arrested for cocaine possession, he said he had to take it in order to get over the news that his girlfriend was dating actors Charlie Sheen and Corey Haim.

....

ARTHUR VALDEZ WAS FOUND

guilty of attempted escape from California's Vacaville prison despite his claims that he was only following instructions from "Domies from the planet Corpus" and had actually "left his body" at the time.

....

AUTHORITIES CHARGED THOMAS

"Tommy Karate" Pitera with being a hit man for the Bonanno organized crime family. Drug Enforcement Administration agents raiding his apartment found hundreds of books on the art of killing, including *How to Kill* (Volumes 1–5), *Silencers, Snipers & Assassins,*

The Hit Man's Handbook, and *Torture, Interrogation and Execution.*

....

SOVIET CHESS STAR VIKTOR

Korchnoi has been playing with former Hungarian grandmaster Geza Maroczy since 1984. Maroczy died in 1951. Korchnoi plays by exchanging moves by phone or mail with a Hungarian medium who is in touch with Maroczy in the afterlife. At the time he was interviewed, about thirty moves into the game, Korchnoi said, "The match started evenly, but Maroczy got into trouble after losing a piece."

....

A WOMAN IN INDIA AGREED TO

grant her husband a divorce in order to marry another woman on condition that he first submit to a public beating administered by her. He agreed and the court allowed it.

....

THE WORLD AS I SEE IT

•••••••••••••••••••••••••••••••

ROBERT BREWSTER OF LONG-

mont, Colorado, sued the United States for the return of much of the northern part of the country, which he claims was given to his ancestors by the King of England. Brewster wants the land back so that he can "form an area where only green-eyed and blue-eyed persons will be permitted." He believes people with such eye color to be superior and in danger of extinction.

•••

FORMER ROMANIAN DICTATOR

Nicolae Ceaucescu once responded to critical anonymous letters written by Romanians to Radio Free Europe by ordering that handwriting samples be taken from the entire population of more than 20 million.

•••

HOLLYWOOD MOVIE MOGUL DON

Simpson told *GQ* magazine that he only wears black Levi's jeans once before getting rid of them. "I like black to be what I call technical black," said Simpson. "One time only and they're out."

....

RICHARD GARY GRIFFING, OF

Mesa, Arizona, a former pesticide salesman, filed papers in the Maricopa County Recorder's Office claiming ownership of the planet Mars and began selling hundred-square-kilometer lots for $19.95. Griffing plans a constitution for the planet that will forbid mobile homes and the singing group Menudo and will make telephone soliciting a capital offense. He said that he will waive landing fees to any United States astronauts.

....

UKRAINIAN ASTRONOMER

Alexei Arkhipov of the Soviet Union's Kharkov Radio-Astronomical Institute believes that he has detected "mysterious sources of radio emissions in the northern part of the sky, near the star Altair." Arkhipov says that the emissions, which he believes are from industrial sources, are about 100 million times stronger than the energy the Earth receives from the Sun. He concludes from this that since it would be impossible for a race to live anywhere near such emissions, then the advanced alien race in question has put all of its industrial output on one planet and lives somewhere else.

....

A FIST-FIGHT BROKE OUT WHEN

sixty traditionalist Roman Catholics tried to take over the main altar at Saint Maclou Cathedral near Paris so that they could celebrate the mass in Latin. The brawl lasted over an hour until a priest agreed to move to a side chapel for his Latin service.

....

ALCIDE CHAISSON, SIXTY-NINE,

was arrested after allegedly standing near the Crystalaire Airport northeast of Los Angeles and using a four-foot-square mirror to attempt to reflect the sun into the eyes of pilots landing planes there. Chaisson claims that the planes drown out the radio in his trailer nearby.

....

RATHER THAN MAKE ANY STATE-

ments, Hakic Ceku appeared in a Spanish courtroom with his lips sewn shut. The man, accused of firearms violations and being part of an armed gang, then attacked his lawyer with a glass ashtray.

....

MASKED MEN KILLED AN EIGHT-

teen-year-old Arab in the West Bank after mistaking him for another man accused of collaborating with the Israelis. They then realized it was the wrong man. They later appeared in the town square using megaphones to tell people that actually the slain youth should be considered a martyr of the Palestinian uprising.

···

ANGERED THAT THE LATE BHIM

Ambedkar, once leader of India's Untouchables, was not portrayed in the movie *Gandhi*, a number of Untouchables released live snakes in a theater showing the film, driving viewers out in a panic.

···

FATHER ELADIO BLANCO,

forty-nine, refused to accompany a funeral procession from his church in Pexeiros-Os Blancos, Spain, to a cemetery, saying, "She [the deceased] has no right to a proper burial because she almost never came to Mass." When the crowd of three hundred mourners insisted, Blanco drew a pistol and fired four shots, wounding one.

···

LOUIS FARRAKHAN, LEADER OF

the Nation of Islam, says he experienced a vision in which a UFO took him from a Mexico mountaintop to a "mother wheel" where the voice of Elijah Muhammad, founder of the religious sect, told him to tell the world that then-President Ronald Reagan was planning a war. Farrakhan said that the later air attack on Libya was partly foiled by the Mother Wheel. "The Wheel was, in fact, present and interfered with the highly sensitive electronic equipment of the aircraft carrier, forcing it to return to Florida for repairs."

....

LISTS

· ·

ANIMAL COLLISIONS

The following have recently been struck by animals:

1. Robert Cooper, forty-eight, killed by a deer, while bicycling in the Great Smoky Mountains National Park in Tennessee.
2. Army Captain Ian Erickson, knocked unconscious by a deer while leading four hundred soldiers on a run at Camp Blanding, Florida.
3. Andrea Spieth, sixteen, knocked down by a deer while skiing at Mount Snow Ski Resort in Vermont.
4. Donald M. Anderson, forty-eight, killed by a bison while snowmobiling in Yellowstone National Park, Wyoming.

··

ANIMAL RESUSCITATION

The following animals were revived by mouth-to-mouth resuscitation:

1. A pair of two-week-old kittens in Durham, North Carolina, by firefighter A. J. Green, after a house fire.
2. A baby kangaroo in Salt Lake City, by state trooper Scott Smith, after a drowning accident.
3. A dalmatian named Willie Wonka in Shelton, Connecticut, by police officer Michael Fusco, after it almost suffocated on a squash ball.

BULLET STOPPERS

The following items stopped bullets in 1990:

1. Beeper, saved the life of a man in Long Beach, California.
2. Pocket radio, prevented a bullet from entering Gary Lee's heart in Los Angeles.
3. Name tag, deflected shot at Tampa, Florida, police officer Thomas Thompson.
4. Back tooth, left Ronnie Ware, fifteen, stunned but okay in Memphis.
5. Dentures, saved Charles Alexander Hinkle, thirty-eight, in Florida.
6. Prayer book, saved security guard Albert Howard, fifty-eight, in Dorset, England.

UPDATES

· ·

LOW SPEED CHASE UPDATE

Mark David Lyman, twenty-four, took Muskogee, Oklahoma, police on a four-mile, hour-and-a-half-long chase never exceeding twenty miles per hour after he stole a construction tractor.

· ·

TWILIGHT ZONE TRAVELER UPDATE

A motorist stopped by police for driving too slowly on the M25 London ring-road asked if he was near Durham, England. The driver had left Kent ten hours earlier and his driving in circles had him nowhere nearer Durham, which was still three hundred miles away.

· ·

TRAPPED UPDATE

Michael Charles Miller, twenty-three, of York, Pennsylvania, was arrested for burglary after firefighters rescued him from the foot-wide rooftop ventilation system of the Horn & Horn Smorgasboard restaurant.

....

Anthropologists at the Smithsonian Institution were able to reconstruct the face of a male skeleton found wearing a woman's dress and stuffed into the chimney of the Good 'N Loud Music store in Madison, Wisconsin, in 1989. Police believe the man was killed elsewhere and hidden in the chimney.

....

NOT DEAD YET UPDATE

Thirteen minutes after being pronounced dead, George Barr, eighty-two, started breathing again. He was released from a Ridgewood, New Jersey, hospital several weeks later and intended to continue working on a series of science books for children.

....

Curt Coleman Clark, twenty-two, was moved to an intensive-care unit of a Winston-Salem, North Carolina, hospital after doctors noticed his foot twitching. He had earlier been pronounced dead, and they were about to begin removing his organs for a donor program.

....

The Saudi Arabian newspaper *al-Riyadh* reported that Muttak Zafer al-Shahrani was dug from his grave twenty-seven hours after burial when shepherds above heard him screaming. Reportedly he had been knocked unconscious on the job and his family had assumed he was dead. He returned home dressed in his burial shroud and both his mother and sister dropped dead from fright at the sight.

....

FOOD FOR
THOUGHT

· ·

JULIA SCHUMANSKY, SIXTY-
four, of Hartsville, Tennessee, underwent surgery for
a tumor in her left buttock. Instead of a tumor, doctors found a four-inch pork chop bone, which they
estimated had been there between five and ten years.

"I couldn't believe it," Schumansky said. "I thought
I was dying from cancer." Describing herself as "over-
weight," she speculated she must have unknowingly
sat on the bone and that the skin grew around it.

· ·

AFTER ARGUING WITH HIS STEP-
sister and hitting her over the head with a gun, Edward Biafore, twenty-nine, barricaded himself inside
his parents' house in Meriden, Connecticut, and announced he wasn't coming out. Armed with a dozen
shotguns and pistols and two hand grenades, he held off

a dozen police officers and a SWAT team for three hours before finally deciding to surrender. Witnesses told police Biafore started the argument over a pizza. His girlfriend, Gina Margery, explained, "He didn't want mushrooms."

....

FOR A SCIENCE PROJECT, TWO

high school students in Beaverton, Oregon, decided to simulate a nuclear explosion. They bought a fresh turkey, then stuffed it with a mixture of six and a half pounds of gunpowder and gasoline. One of the boys was using the powder to make a thirty-foot fuse, but it flashed and burned him. The other boy called the rescue squad, which then summoned the bomb squad to dispose of the bird. Bomb experts blew it up, sending a plume of smoke and turkey parts about two hundred feet in the air.

....

A MAN TRIED TO STICK UP A

cafe in Montpelier, France, with a candy revolver, but the owner saw it was a fake and called police. By the time they arrived, the man had eaten the weapon.

....

ACCORDING TO SHERIFF'S DEPU-

ties in LaPlace, Louisiana, Jarmaine Gardner, eighteen, shot Troy Joseph Dropthmore, nineteen, in a dispute at a buffet. "I was in line getting food, and he said, 'You're taking it all,' even though there was a lot more left," Dropthmore recalled after doctors removed a bullet lodged near his spine. "Then he said, 'You're taking all day,' I turned around—and boom."

In Augusta, Georgia, Dale Brantley Peeler was sitting at a fast-food restaurant drive-through checking his order, according to witnesses, when the driver behind him blew his horn. After Peeler and the driver both got out and exchanged words, the passenger in the second vehicle got out and shot Peeler dead.

....

WHEN CZECHOSLOVAKIA DO-

nated 2,800 cans of beef to Zambia in 1990, tests showed the meat was radioactive, so authorities buried the cans twelve feet underground and covered the site with a concrete slab. That didn't deter hungry Zambians, who used pick axes to dig them up. "I can assure you this meat we have been having in the past one month," declared scavenger Mubita Sililo on behalf of himself and his wife, "is the best we have ever had since we married."

A similar incident occurred in Brazil two years earlier. Health authorities there seized five tons of decomposed meat and buried it ten feet deep at a trash dump. To prevent scavenging, the authorities mixed it in with hospital waste. Still, hundreds of hungry slum dwellers flocked to the dump and dug it up.

....

STATE HEALTH DEPARTMENT IN-

spectors in Provo, Utah, fined Evan Hansen, twenty-three, $500 for violating Utah's Water Pollution Control Act by illegally dumping one thousand pounds of raspberry gelatin and sixteen gallons of whipped cream. Hansen still came out $4,500 ahead. He won $5,000 for the most outrageous stunt in a contest at a local shopping center by cutting the roof from a station wagon and filling it with gelatin and whipped cream.

After the contest, he found it was going to cost him too much money to have someone come pump the goo away. So he simply opened the doors of the car and let the melting mess spill down the parking lot storm drain. After finding red globs mixing with leaves and twigs in a creek that the drain empties into, health department officials tracked Hansen down and issued the fine.

....

OFFICIALS AT THE HALL PRISON

outside Stockholm reported the escape of a skinny inmate who saved all the margarine from his meals until he had enough to cover himself and squeeze through the bars.

....

FLOYD YULLIE, SEVENTY-TWO,

king of the fourth Irregular Prune Parade in El Monte, California, failed to appear at the event after he became ill from eating too many prunes.

....

HIJACKINGS AND CRASHES

aren't the biggest risks airline passengers face, according to a 1989 British study. Food poisoning is. Nearly 25 percent of all airline meals inspected contained ten times permitted bacteria levels. The study acknowledged that, although food poisoning already is the top cause of pilot illness, fewer than thirty outbreaks of airline food poisoning have been reported in the past twenty-five years, but insisted that such incidents are grossly underreported.

MENSA
REJECTS
· ·

IN MASSACHUSETTS, THE PITTS-
field School Committee announced that students could
fulfill their physical education requirement by reading pamphlets about exercise.

· ·

AS VARIOUS STATE AND FED-
eral courts had four previous times, a U.S. court denied an appeal by William Jefferson Walker, who was
sentenced in 1983 to serve ten years in an Arizona
prison for aggravated assault. Walker's petition argued that he was deprived of a fair trial because no
one in his jury pool had a last name that began with
W, X, Y, or Z. Walker claimed that people with
surnames late in the alphabet have an increased tend-
ency toward "alphabetic neurosis," a mental condition brought on "by the constant strain of waiting for

one's name to be reached in the classroom and in other situations." Walker derived his theory from a scientific article that actually found little evidence to support the idea.

....

WHEN LOUISIANA TRIED TO

raise its educational standards in the late 1980s, many high school students began dropping out, then enrolling in GED programs, which are designed for adults who have been out of school a while and which generally have lower standards. GED programs accounted for 20 percent of Louisiana's high school diplomas in 1988, and the state's dropout rate was estimated at 40 percent.

....

WHEN A SAN MATEO COUNTY,

California, sheriff's deputy approached Barry Buchstaber, who was standing beside a car with two broken windows, and asked for identification, Buchstaber handed the deputy the only official document he had—a copy of a current arrest warrant against him for driving with a suspended license.

....

A GUEST AT A PARTY IN KIN-

caid, West Virginia, was trying to explode a blasting cap, hooked to a battery, in an aquarium. When it wouldn't go off, another guest, Jerry Stromyer, twenty-four, said he would demonstrate how to do it. He put the blasting cap in his mouth and bit down, blowing out all his teeth and extensively injuring his tongue and lips.

....

DAVID ASHLEY, CHARGED WITH

raising poultry without a permit, appeared in court in Seneca Falls, New York, with a rooster tucked under his arm. When village justice Gordon Tetor ordered the bird removed, Ashley told the judge that the bird was his attorney, explaining "it was the only legal counsel I could afford."

....

POLICE IN LEWISBURG, TENNES-

see, spotted a ten-gallon tub of marijuana plants but couldn't spare any officers to watch for the owner. They confiscated the plants and printed a picture of them in the Lewisburg *Tribune* with the caption: "Have you lost a tub of marijuana? If you have, you may claim it at the Lewisburg Police Department." Police arrested Leroy Chilton, twenty-six, when he appeared and said the plants were his.

....

THREE TEENAGERS TOOK ADVAN-

tage of New Jersey Transit's free-ride offer on its Morris and Essex rail line. After the conductor collected the coupons and went into the next car, the three spotted his briefcase and took the contents: train tickets and about $50 in cash. At the next stop, the conductor returned for his briefcase, saw the youths with his briefcase, and chased them. They fled the train, but the conductor checked the free-ride coupons they had given him and found their names and addresses. He notified New Jersey Transit Police, who greeted them at their homes and recovered the stolen items.

....

IN WATERBURY, CONNECTICUT,

Superior Court Judge Maxwell J. Heiman sentenced Richard C. Dobbins, Jr., to ten days in jail and fined him $100 for causing himself and sixty-six others in the jury pool to be disqualified from a triple-murder trial. When the court clerk called the roll of prospective jurors, each answered "Here," except Dobbins, who yelled "Guilty!"

....

THOMAS L. MARTIN, TWENTY-

two, manager of a Jack-in-the-Box restaurant in Oroville, California, reported that he was robbed of $307 after work. He provided police sketch artist Sergeant Jack Lee with a detailed description of the subject. After Lee finished the drawing, he observed "it looked just like Martin." Police arrested Martin, who confessed to taking the money himself.

....

THE INTERNAL REVENUE SER-

vice charged Curtis and Denise Nall with filing 978 fictitious income tax returns asking for more than $1 million in refunds. The IRS uncovered the scheme after scores of phony returns, each bearing false W-2 forms and asking for refunds of $1,052, arrived at ten IRS centers around the country. All the returns were completed in the names of Robert A. and Mary C. Smith, were postmarked Greensboro, North Carolina, and asked that refunds be sent to a post office box in the Bahamas.

....

THANKS
FOR NOTHING
• •

WHEN CALIFORNIA STATE UNI-
versity at Northridge replaced traditional toggle-style
light switches in 180 campus offices with energy-saving
switches that work by automatically shutting off the
lights any time they fail to detect motion, professors
complained. James Sefton, for instance, said he had
to get up from his chair ten times in three hours and
wave to convince the switch he was there. His col-
league Max Lupal noted: "There was a woman across
the hall engaging in all sorts of gymnastics in her
office to keep the light on."

• •

CANADIAN TOURISTS ERIC
Plourde, nineteen, and Patrick Chartrand, twenty,
who had driven from California to New York, stopped
their car in the Bensonhurst section of Brooklyn when

they saw a woman in her mid-eighties sprawled on the sidewalk, calling for help. After they got out to assist her, they were attacked by a group of ten to twelve teen-agers wielding bats and pipes who police said apparently thought the Canadians were mugging the woman.

....

NEW YORK STATE TROOPER JO-

seph Cyran, bicycling from Los Angeles to Atlantic City to raise money for drunk-driving victims, was forty miles short of his goal when he was struck and critically injured by a drunk driver.

....

THE CITY OF VIENNA COMMIS-

sioned Austrian sculptor Alfred Hrdlicka to modify a statue of a prostrate Jew that commemorates the Holocaust because tourists were using the bronze figure as a park bench or picnic table. Hrdlicka solved the problem by embedding the bronze figure with barbed wire.

....

WHEN YITZHAK KRASILTCHIK

left the Soviet Union for Israel, he was met at Jerusalem's Ben Gurion Airport by Absorption Minister Yitzhak Peretz, who welcomed him as Israel's hundred thousandth immigrant and whisked the eighty-seven-year-old man and his family of four away in a limousine to the arrivals lounge, where children serenaded him. When the greeting ceremony ended and the dignitaries had left, the Krasiltchiks discovered they had missed the bus to their new home in the southern Negev Desert. What's more, they were the only people left at the airport and had nowhere to stay.

....

AS WAS ITS CUSTOM, LAKE-
land, Florida, rewarded city employee James Moran for his twenty years of service with a service pin and a certificate for a free dinner for two. Other workers had spent $34 to $60, but Moran and his fiancée ran up a $511 tab. His angry superiors suspended him for two weeks and demoted him to a position that paid $11,000 a year less. Moran eventually paid the bill, but an appeal board upheld the demotion.

....

IN CHIPPEWA FALLS, WISCON-
sin, Thomas L. Weber announced that financial problems forced him to close the office that was the center for a project to raise $25 million to build a reception station for visitors from outer space. His plan called for the station to provide a safe landing area for aliens. Weber had counted on a groundswell of financial support and said he did get "tens of thousands of

159

letters." Most of the letters contained no money, however, just requests for more information, which Weber couldn't afford the postage to answer.

....

A NEW YORK APPEALS COURT

ruled that a judge should have declared a mistrial when a doctor accused of malpractice saved the life of a juror in front of the rest of the jury. Even though the jury found the defendant, Dr. Ho Woon Lee, liable for damages, it awarded the plaintiff only $3,500 for medical expenses and $10,000 for pain and suffering. The Supreme Court's Appellate Division said the "unconscionably low award suggests that the jury was subliminally influenced to view Lee favorably at [the defendant's] expense."

....

A WOMAN IN LUEBBEN, EAST

Germany, divorced her husband in 1982 because he helped so much around the house that she had nothing to do. The woman told the court that at first she considered him a "dream of a husband" because he did everything perfectly—cooking, baking, housecleaning, washing up, shopping, taking care of the baby, even washing the windows. "But after a while it drove me mad," she said. "What was left for me to do?"

....

WHEN A COMMUNIST PARTY PA-

per in China hailed Wang Zaoming in 1985 for successfully breeding a new flower, people either wrote her asking for seeds, saplings, or outright cash, or else they dropped by her home to ask in person. She finally collapsed from the strain of cooking an average of seven dinners daily for visitors, who also walked off with six hundred pots of flowers.

....

ODD ENDINGS

· ·

ADOLPH DAXBOECK, TWENTY-

three, was taking part in a contest in Burnaby, British Columbia, to see how far a Ping-Pong ball could be blown. He inhaled by mistake, and the ball lodged in his throat, choking him to death.

· ·

CHARLES W. DOAK, OWNER OF

the Wilson Candy Company in Rocky Mount, North Carolina, was killed during a robbery after being hit on the head several times by a nine-pound, two-and-a-half-foot candy cane.

· ·

IN PAKISTAN, NOOR ALAM,

sixty, bought a cow to sacrifice in a Muslim festival.

While letting it graze, he made a loop in the rope holding the cow and put it around his neck to free his hands. The cow ran away, dragging Alam quite a distance and fatally injuring him.

· ·

AFTER TELLING HIS WIFE HE

was unable to bear the pain caused by angina, Joe Boothroyd, seventy-one, of Chichester, England, committed suicide by drilling a hole in his heart.

· ·

ARMY RESERVE PARACHUTIST

Pfc. Martin Askew was killed in Anne Arundel County, Maryland, after a routine jump went bad and the soldier landed in a pool of liquified manure just outside the drop zone.

A similar fate befell Monica K. Myers, mayor of Betterton, Maryland, who slipped and fell into a tank of human waste at the town's waste-water treatment plant.

· ·

SETH DANIELS OF CAREFREE,

Arizona, died while landing his glider in the desert near Phoenix. A wing clipped a twenty-foot cactus, causing it to fall on the glider's cockpit, crushing Daniels.

· ·

IN DRAPERSTOWN, NORTHERN

Ireland, Charles Rogers, sixty-seven, was watching a grave being dug for his dead brother when the sides started to cave in. He reached down to help a grave-digger and fell himself. When he hit the bottom, the headstone fell on top of him, crushing him.

....

JASON GOLDFARB, SEVENTEEN,

a junior at Nashoba Regional High School in Massachusetts, climbed a soccer goalpost with some other students to place a memorial on top of it in remembrance of two schoolmates killed a day before in an auto accident. The five-hundred-pound goalpost toppled, causing the students to fall off, then fell on top of Goldfarb, fatally injuring him.

....

OFFICIALS IN LIANELLI, WALES,

said that fisherman Bernard Maunder died because he wore hip boots out into the surf. When he found himself trapped by a rising tide, the boots filled with water and pulled him to his death before rescuers could reach him.

....

FIRST THINGS
FIRST

• •

ALBERT MANGINO OF NEW CAS-

tle, Pennsylvania, was sentenced to thirty-two days behind bars for drunken driving in 1987, but because he claimed he gambled on horses for a living, Common Pleas Judge Ralph Pratt granted him work release status so he could leave jail each day to go to a West Virginia racetrack.

AN ARMED MAN ENTERED A BAR

in Cedar Rapids, Iowa, in 1976 and announced, "Don't anybody move." The customers, who were watching the *CBS Morning News,* paid no attention, except for one who said, "Nobody is getting robbed while I'm watching the news," and accused the gunman of bluffing. Next, the bartender said, the gunman cocked his pistol twice, but nobody reacted. "You aren't taking this seriously," the man complained and ran out the door, saying he was going to get some friends and come back. Before he did, police arrested him.

....

AS PUBLIC-TELEVISION VIEWERS

in twelve cities sat glued to their sets while doctors in Philadelphia reconstructed fifteen-month-old Michele Miller's skull during a two-hour operation broadcast live, the girl's parents, Lynn and Paul Miller of Princeton, New Jersey, opted to watch *The Wizard of Oz* instead.

....

EIGHT INMATES BROKE OUT OF

their cells at the Nashville, Tennessee, city jail. While trying to escape, they found themselves in the women's cellblock. Distracted, they forgot about escaping and engaged in sex with female inmates until guards tracked them down and apprehended them.

....

BEFORE THE START OF THE

Persian Gulf war, Israel's Chief Rabbi Mordechai Eliyahu ruled that ultra-Orthodox Jewish men could break Jewish law forbidding men from shaving in case of an Iraqi chemical attack so gas masks could fit properly over their beards. Eliyahu urged bearded men to carry scissors in their pocket in case they needed to shave quickly.

Also, although Jewish law regarding the Sabbath

forbids even simple physical activities, such as turning on the radio, the threat of Iraqi missile attacks once the war started sent Israel's chief rabbis scrambling to the Scriptures for a loophole so Orthodox Jews could listen to the news for warnings. The rabbis ruled that leaving the radio on during the Sabbath was permissible—provided it was on low volume. "If there is a real alarm, you can turn up the volume, but in a nonconventional manner, with a stick or with your elbow," explained Religious Affairs Minister Avner Shaki. "Controlling the volume in a different manner still marks the Sabbath as different from the rest of the week."

....

NOTING THE HIGH COST OF SAV-

ing premature babies and the likelihood that the ones who do survive suffer lifelong health problems, Stanford University researchers David Stevenson and Ernie W. D. Young said doctors should let extremely small preemies die. They said that the $2.6 billion a year neonatal care in the United States costs would be better spent addressing "the root causes of prematurity."

....

AT A MAXIMUM-SECURITY STATE

prison in Shirley, Massachusetts, Gordon Benjamin III was granted parole but decided to remain behind bars for another two months to appear as Sir Lancelot in an inmate production of *Camelot*. The cast had already lost four King Arthurs, two Merlins, and one

Squire Dap before opening night because prisoners playing these roles were transferred.

....

A 1985 BILL THAT PROPOSED LE-

galizing prostitution in Washington state provided that licenses be issued "only upon satisfactory proof that the applicant is of good character."

....

LEONA AND LARRY COTTAM OF

Wilkes-Barre, Pennsylvania, were charged with third-degree murder in the starvation of their fourteen-year-old son, Eric. Authorities say the whole family of four went hungry for six weeks rather than buy food with the only money they had—more than $3,500 set aside as a religious tithe.

....

IN MICHIGAN, ALGER COUNTY

Circuit Court Judge Charles Stark sentenced convicted rapist David Caballero to pay $975 in court costs and $200 compensation to the victim and serve three years' probation, after which the conviction would be removed from his record. Stark explained he gave Caballero the lenient sentence because a conviction would have prevented the twenty-one-year-old college student, a criminal justice major, from achieving his goal of becoming a police officer.

....

IN CHICAGO, THREE MONTHS

after winning a free college education for persevering over inner-city hardship to become a model student, high school senior Eva Garcia was arrested for the murder of her forty-one-year-old husband. According to police, a few weeks before being named to receive the scholarship, Garcia secretly married Louie Weber. Once she won the award, however, she conspired to murder him because she feared the marriage would stand in the way of her future.

....

ON THE JOB

. . . .

WHEN ONLY THIRTY-SEVEN PEO-
ple showed up at a conference to which five thousand
had been invited, French Tourism Minister Olivier Stirn
hired two hundred local actors to sit in the audience
while twelve government ministers and two former
prime ministers spoke. Believing they got off work at
6:15 P.M., however, all two hundred stood up during
Defense Minister Jean Pierre Chevenement's talk and
walked out.

. . . .

POLICE IN NORWALK, CONNECTI-
cut, charged a bank teller with robbing another bank
just up the street on his lunch hour. According to
Lieutenant Arthur Arway, Michael McKenna, thirty-

seven, "punched out, robbed the bank, went home and left the money, and punched back in."

· ·

TO PREVENT RESIDENTS OF

Myerstown, Pennsylvania, from thinking that borough offices were empty in case they called while workers were using the lavatory, Borough Manager Ed Treat installed phones in the restrooms.

· ·

MAFIA GANGSTERS SUFFER

worse stress than top business executives, according to Dr. Granesco Aragora. The Sicilian pathologist, who spent more than forty years studying Mafiosi remains, concluded that gangsters tend to have "thickened arteries, kidney failure, stomach ulcers," and livers that are "yellowish, fatty, and chronically short of glucose."

· ·

BUDGET CUTS AT THE PAWNEE

County, Nebraska, Sheriff's Department prompted Sheriff John Schulze to install a telephone answering machine to handle evening and weekend emergency calls.

· ·

THE VATICAN ANNOUNCED IN 1989

that Pope John Paul II was hiring additional exorcists to fight the increase in demonic possessions.

....

IN TAMPA, FLORIDA, IVETTE

Gonzalez sued her former employer, the Salvation Army, for forbidding her to speak Spanish at work—even though her ability to speak Spanish helped her get the job in the first place. Gonzalez said the English-only rule went into effect two months after she started. Carroll Hepperle, director of the center where Gonzalez worked, said the rule was necessary because some employees heard others speaking Spanish and felt they were being talked about.

....

DONATO CAUSARANO, FIFTY-

three, a court clerk in San Giovanni Valdarno, Italy, was working alone late at night when he reached for some documents and a stack of files fell on him, trapping him for five hours.

....

A 1990 RETROSPECTIVE OF DAN

Rather's career as CBS news anchor by *The Washington Times* included these highlights:

• Refusing to sit in predecessor Walter Cronkite's chair

on his first show, anchoring "contorted in a kind of squat"
- Wearing a sweater under his coat for better ratings and reintroducing it when ratings fell
- Beginning to sign off with "Courage!" in September 1986 (and "coraje" in Spanish), then abruptly stopping after a week
- Refusing to pay a $12.50 taxi fare in Chicago, then being shanghaied by the driver
- Being punched out by an unidentified man at a CBS affiliates' convention
- Being beaten up by men asking, "Kenneth, what is the frequency?"
- Telling *The New York Times* he always carries *The Elements of Style* with him, on advice of Eric Sevareid, then telling another writer he never read the book
- Parroting a Soviet press release that AIDS was developed in a U.S. Army lab
- Refusing to go on the air for six minutes during a 1987 newscast because a tennis match had run over
- Becoming so unnerved by NBC anchor Tom Brokaw's presence at a party that he refused to shake a CBS executive's hand and instead planted a "wet kiss" on him
- Insinuating in an on-air interview that former CIA Director William Casey was still alive
- Losing an on-air confrontation with George Bush in January 1988 that was responsible for Bush shedding his wimp image

··

LIN CHAN, FIFTY, WAS APPOINT-
ed birth control consultant to women living in China's

remote northern provinces in 1984, even though she had fifteen children of her own.

....

DEACONS OF THE GREEK ORTHO-
dox Church in Athens demanded a 15 percent pay raise in 1985 to compensate them for having to inhale incense smoke during services. They complained it was as bad as cigarette smoke.

....

NEW THEORIES
OF RELATIVITY
· ·

IN BOYNTON BEACH, FLORIDA,
Mary Grieco, forty-eight, her fifteen-year-old daughter Ann, and the daughter's sometime boyfriend, Melvin Steele, nineteen, confessed to police that they shot Joe Grieco, fifty-two, to death. They claimed he was a miserable, grouchy man who spent most of his life lying on the couch watching television. Ann Grieco explained that she and her mother decided to kill him as a last resort only because her parents couldn't afford a divorce.

· ·

AFTER PHOEBE SCHNEIDER OF
Carteret, New Jersey, sued her husband Eugene for divorce in 1976, she filed a second suit charging that he went too far in dividing their property equally. She

alleged that he used a chain saw to cut their home in half, rendering it uninhabitable.

....

IN MEMPHIS, JUVENILE JUDGE
Kenneth Turner ordered a psychiatric examination for a thirteen-year-old boy who chopped off his uncle's hand at the uncle's request.

....

AN APPEALS COURT IN SAINT
Louis denied a request by Steven Goodwin, thirty-four, an inmate at the federal prison in Springfield, Missouri, that prison officials provide a container for his semen, which would be rushed to his thirty-year-old wife so that she could have his baby. The three-judge panel said that granting Goodwin's request would be too burdensome and costly. Judge Frank J. Magill commented, "If the [Bureau of Prisons] were forced to allow male prisoners to procreate, whatever the means, it would have to confer a corresponding benefit to its female prisoners."

....

A THIRTY-FOUR-YEAR-OLD NEW
Haven, Connecticut, man charged with shaking his three-month-old daughter to death believed that she hated him, according to court records, and wore a Jimmy Carter mask to keep her from crying whenever he approached her.

....

MARY AYALA OF WALNUT, CALI-

fornia, explained that her sole reason for getting pregnant at age forty-three was to provide a bone-marrow donor for her teenage daughter, who doctors said was dying of leukemia.

....

ACCORDING TO POLICE IN POM-

pano Beach, Florida, Christopher Morris plotted with his parents to kill his ex-wife to collect $35,000 in insurance. When they found out that the policy had lapsed, the parents killed Morris instead to collect on a $70,000 policy. Police said Theron and Leila Mary Morris also were angry that their forty-two-year-old ex-convict son sold them bogus cocaine for $1,000 that they had intended to resell. The couple and Martin Rector, their son's roommate and one-time prison buddy who was accused of being the triggerman, then conned a drifter with drinking and blackout problems into confessing to the crime.

....

IN WOOD COUNTY, KENTUCKY,

Rhoda Maddox, thirty-nine, pleaded guilty to setting fire to her mother's home December 27, 1985, and killing seven members of her family. She set the fire after becoming upset that her mother gave her brother a videocassette recorder for Christmas but gave her knitting yarn.

Briton George Bangs, fifty-nine, was convicted in Exeter Crown Court for setting his house on fire. He explained that he was driven mad by his wife's constant organ playing. "If you have someone playing the organ twenty-four hours a day, seven days a week, how would you react?" he said, noting, "She didn't play that well, either."

And in a suburb of Bogotá, Colombia, Luis Alfonso Borda became enraged when he found out his wife had not washed his shirt. He went out to the garage, got thirteen sticks of dynamite, and was preparing to blow up the house when police arrived.

....

MARYLAND STATE POLICE AR-

rested Charles L. Brockway in connection with the death of his wife, Valerie A. Brockway. Investigators say the Baltimore couple were sitting in a restaurant on Tilghman Island, when they began arguing. Brockway was accused of leaving the restaurant, getting into his van, and driving it through the restaurant window, striking his wife.

And in Newark, New Jersey, a lawyer who did marital counseling with her police-officer husband used a Jaguar XJ6 to kill him. According to investigators, Olivia and Frank Howard, who were married for twenty years, met for lunch. Both were in the car when Frank Howard got out. Olivia then pursued him for at least two blocks, driving the wrong way down a one-way street before knocking him down and running him over.

....

MAHMOUD AYAZI, THIRTY-ONE,

an Iranian citizen who had lived in Sacramento, California, for more than five years, returned to Iran and married Kataun Safaie, twenty. The couple flew to Frankfurt, West Germany, where Ayazi tried to get a visa for his bride. After being told it could take up to a year, he decided to smuggle her to the United States in a piece of baggage. Arriving in Los Angeles, Ayazi claimed the suitcase but discovered that Safaie was dead, apparently because of the weight of the other luggage thrown on top of her suitcase, according to the authorities. They added that the distraught Ayazi returned to Sacramento and shot himself in the head.

....

CHARLES BARBER, FIFTY-ONE,
traveled from Las Vegas to Huntington, West Virginia, to visit his dying mother. After two weeks of caring for her, he argued with his brother Larry, fifty-three, who, according to police, had a drinking problem and did little to help. Following the argument, Larry Barber killed his brother with a shotgun.

....

OOPS!

• •

TO DEMONSTRATE A NEW IN-
sect repellent at a restaurant in London, Diana Moran,
a star of a British television fitness show, climbed
into a glass cage with more than three thousand
starved mosquitoes. The mosquitoes escaped, however, and attacked the audience of businessmen and
journalists, leaving them bitten, swollen, and itching.
Moran, the only person protected by the new repellent, wasn't bitten.

• •

SHIRLEY KOOTA, SIXTY-TWO, OF
Miami accompanied her husband Bert, sixty-five, to a
pistol range to learn how to use their new .22 automatic. During the lesson, she squeezed off a round,
and the hot cartridge, ejected by the pistol, flew down

the front of her dress. It startled her so badly that she whirled around and shot Bert in the leg.

....

IN LAFAYETTE, CALIFORNIA, A

five-hundred-pound corpse that had to be sent through the crematory twice caused a chimney to overheat, according to five department officials, setting off a fire that caused $100,000 worth of damage.

In Lusby, Maryland, Darlene Bowman found a black snake outside her bathroom and called a neighbor for help. The neighbor poured gasoline on the nonpoisonous snake, but the vapors were ignited by the pilot light of a furnace about ten feet away. According to fire officials, the fire killed the snake but caused $50,000 damage.

Finally, at a dress rehearsal of *The Nutcracker Suite* by the Wisconsin Dance Ensemble, a live rabbit being pulled from a flaming dish caught fire when burning fluid ignited its coat, sending it fleeing across the stage and causing the group to drop plans to perform the magic trick during performances.

....

TWO WEEKS AFTER KENTUCKY

businessman Charles Hayes paid $45 to buy a used computer system from the U.S. attorney's office in Lexington, the office informed him that the system's memory might not have been erased and could contain sealed grand jury indictments, information about federally protected witnesses and FBI informants, and data about employees in U.S. Attorney Louis DeFalaise's office.

....

POLICE IN EVANSVILLE, INDI-

ana, rescued Raymond O'Neal, fifty-eight, from a re-
clining chair, where he had fallen face-first and been
stuck for at least twenty-four hours, according to neighbors. They heard yells from O'Neal's duplex but were
unable to get him to answer the door or telephone, so
they called the police, who figured he fell and became
trapped when his arm lodged in the chair. "His head
was right about where the headrest is," Patrolman
Tom Pfender said. "His forearm and wrist were in
between the cushion and armrest." O'Neal didn't recall how he got stuck.

About the same time in West Lafayette, Indiana,
Stephen D. Phipps, thirty, spent four days with his
head pinned between a dresser and the floor in his
apartment before police found him. Neighbors said
they had heard moaning coming from Phipps's apartment but said that it was not unusual.

....

WHEN THE ARMY TESTED A NEW

air-defense gun called the Sergeant York, which
was designed to home in on the whirling blades of
helicopters and propeller-driven aircraft, it ignored
the chopper targets. Instead, the weapon demolished
a ventilating fan on a nearby latrine.

....

A FEATURE OF A 1985 SOVIET

trade show was an "exhibition of shame and disgrace," designed to embarrass producers of defective

merchandise. A prime example was a large shipment of women's boots with high heels—attached to the toe.

....

HAROLD WOMACK'S PORSCHE GOT

stuck in a cinder pit at the Sunset Crater National Monument, and the fifty-one-year-old Phoenix, Arizona, man thought he could get it out by using a 20-ton steamroller he spotted nearby. Womack drove the steamroller over to his car and hopped off to attach a chain, but the machine kept rolling and flattened Womack's car.

....

A HOUSE IN CHESTER, PENNSYL-

vania, exploded when a deliveryman dumped fifty-eight gallons of fuel oil into the basement by mistake. The home had been converted to gas heat, but the old oil-filler pipe on the outside of the house remained. The fuel oil was supposed to have been delivered to another house a block away. The occupants of the house escaped unharmed, but a woman standing near the house when it exploded was critically injured. According to a neighbor, when the explosion occurred the deliveryman cut the oil hose from his truck and drove away.

....

FRUITS OF
RESEARCH

· ·

A STUDY OF OVINE SEXUALITY

by University of California at Davis graduate student
Anne Perkins noted the difficulty of determining if
lesbianism exists among sheep "because if you are a
female sheep, what you do to solicit sex is stand still.
Maybe there is a female sheep out there really want-
ing another female, but there's just no way for us to
know it."

· ·

THE UNIVERSITY OF TOKYO'S

medical department has collected at least 120 brains
of prime ministers, novelists, artists, and scholars
since 1913 to determine what makes the brains of
famous people special. "We'd like to get many more,"
said Yutaka Yoshida, the collection's curator. "I'd es-

pecially like to get brains from mathematicians, musicians, and singers."

About the only thing scientists have been able to conclude from the collection is that the brains of some famous people were heavier than those of less distinguished thinkers. Detailed examinations of the brains have been limited because of the deep-rooted Japanese reluctance to tamper with the dead. "We try, as far as possible, not to cut them," Yoshida said. "We want to keep them in their original shape." He admitted, however, "You can't do much research, just looking at the outside of the brains."

. . . .

TEXAS A&M CHEMISTRY PRO-

fessor Don Sawyer announced he had developed a commercial process to turn toxic waste into salt.

. . . .

THE AIR FORCE ANNOUNCED IT

was funding a $100,000 project at the University of Florida to blast simulated jet engines through barns to see how the noise affects pregnant horses.

. . . .

THE *NEW ENGLAND JOURNAL OF*

Medicine warned that communion wafers often used in Catholic and Anglican services might be hazardous. The report noted the wafers are made from wheat flour containing gluten and other substances that can prompt an attack of a digestive disorder that prevents the absorption of nutrients and causes a variety of symptoms.

Meanwhile, Australian physician Dr. Margaret T. Taylor traced an eight-year-old girl's lead poisioning to the rosary beads the girl was in the habit of kissing. Taylor suggested that lead poisoning from the same source could account for anemia among nuns and other devout Catholics.

....

CITING THE EXAMPLE OF LEON-

ardo da Vinci, sleep expert Claudio Stampi of the Institute of Circadian Physiology in Boston announced that people can get by on only ninety minutes of sleep a day if they limit themselves to fifteen-minute naps every four hours. He did note that one Italian actor who emulated the Renaissance artist's sleep schedule had to quit after six months because he had too much spare time. "He didn't know what to do with it," Stampi said, "since he wasn't another Leonardo."

....

SEX IS ITS OWN PUNISHMENT

• •

TWO NEW YORK STATE MAINTE-

nance workers were dismissed after their supervisors videotaped them having sex after working hours on another worker's desk. The supervisors set up the video camera after the other worker complained that his desk smelled like it was being used for sex.

AFTER A COUPLE WAS SEEN SIM-

ulating sex inside a helicopter hovering outside the windows of the Club Hotel in Tiberias, Israel as part of a New Year's Party at the hotel, the city's chief rabbi revoked the hotel's kosher license.

THE MARYLAND COURT OF AP-

peals ruled that Silvio Figueredo-Torres, forty-nine,

could proceed with his $10 million suit against Bethesda psychologist Herbert J. Nickel for malpractice and intentionally inflicting emotional distress; to wit, having an affair with Figueredo-Torres's wife. Nickel denied having sex with Marsha Figueredo-Torres, fifty, during therapy or before she separated from her husband, although just after the couple divorced he did marry her.

Silvio Figueredo-Torres's suit charges Nickel with demoralizing him by ridiculing him and telling him to stay away from his wife. During therapy, Nickel called him "a codfish" and said his wife deserved a "fillet." Nickel told the husband that he had bad breath and was to blame for the couple's problems.

FLORIDA'S DEPARTMENT OF

Natural Resources recommended banning tourist attractions where customers pay to get into the water with captive bottle-nosed dolphins. It cited reports of adult male dolphins becoming sexually aroused and making sexual overtures to humans, including physical aggression and other aspects of the mammals' mating ritual.

In one incident, a legal secretary from Miami said that soon after she entered the water, she noticed one seven-hundred-pound dolphin rubbing against her in an unmistakably amorous way. She recalled, "He liked me a lot."

WHEN COUNTY SUPERVISORS

threatened its budget, Nassau Community College in

Hempstead, New York, agreed to modify a controversial course on sexuality. College officials axed visits to gay bars, interviews with prostitutes, eighty slides of male and female genitalia, and such homework assignments as masturbating while taking a bubble bath. The college said students still would see an explicit film on sexual intercourse.

....

DR. ROCHELLE KONITS, FORTY-

one, was arrested and charged with plotting to have a male doctor drugged, kidnapped, and brought to her Long Island apartment so she could fulfill a sexual fantasy. She unwittingly hired an undercover narcotics agent and a police informant—who were already investigating her for dispensing drugs without medical treatment—to carry out the kidnapping, according to Nassau County Assistant District Attorney James DiPietro, who noted the two were to receive $500 and future prescriptions for Valium. "You may have to knock him out first using your fists," she reportedly told the two in a tape-recorded conversation. "Get him back here. I'm not going to hurt him, but I'm going to kill him with love."

....

BRITISH ZOOS ANNOUNCED IN

1985 that they would cease training chimpanzees to mimic humans at tea parties, which they had staged for years to attract visitors, because the practice was ruining the animals' sex lives. Researchers said the animals become so involved with aping human behavior that they lose interest in their own kind. The result was a dramatic drop in the birth rate at the nation's zoos.

....

ATTORNEYS FOR ACCUSED BIGA-

mist Air Force Captain Neil Clark explained their client agreed to marry the second woman in order to sleep with her because his overwhelming sexual desire diminished his mental capacity.

....

IN SPRING LAKE, MICHIGAN,

students in a high-school health class were assigned to carry a five-pound sack of flour for three days without leaving it unattended to learn what it's like to have a child that needs constant attention. Problems arose when some students not enrolled in the course began "killing" the flour babies between classes. According to Marybeth Lobbezo, coordinator of the reproductive health unit, ninety of the flour babies suffered stab wounds, fifty were the objects of death threats, forty-one were kidnapped, eighty were harassed, and fifty-one were murdered. "It was a response we hadn't anticipated," Lobbezo said.

....

NUTS BEHIND THE WHEEL

· ·

IN SEATTLE, GEORGE FUREDI,
thirty-seven, was charged with driving his car up the
steps of a Mormon church and through the door. He
explained that the church's public address system
kept him awake at night.

· ·

IN THE LOS ANGELES SUBURB OF
Canoga Park, John A. Anderson, seventy-two, was
picking up an examiner to take his driving test when
the car lurched forward. It crashed through the wall
of the Department of Motor Vehicles building, ca-
reened through the counter area, and came to rest
thirty feet inside the building, but not before sending

some sixty people scrambling, injuring six office workers, and causing $40,000 worth of damage.

···

MICHAEL LANE, TWENTY-EIGHT,

of Providence, Rhode Island, was arrested for driving his car through the front doors of Saint Joseph Hospital and plowing into the information desk in the lobby, apparently to get immediate attention for two passengers who had been stabbed.

···

POLICE ARRESTED EMMET

Wheat, forty-seven, in the San Francisco suburb of Hayward, California, for hitting eighteen vehicles with his flatbed truck, injuring twelve people. His wife, Karen, said she spoke to him over the truck's two-way radio just before he crashed into the highway center divider after littering three miles of the Nimitz Freeway with dented vehicles. "He said the Lord had spoken to him," Karen Wheat recounted, "and that the Lord told him he could drive through cars."

···

POLICE IN KASSEL, WEST GER-

many, checking a car abandoned after an accident, found its windshield washer bottle full of schnapps and a tube leading directly to the dashboard. When police tracked down the driver, he admitted that he had been taking swigs of the liquor from the tube before the crash.

....

WHEN PATROLMAN PHILIP

Human spotted three children riding in the open truck of a sedan in Nyack, New York, he stopped the car and found eight more people were riding in the front seat—five over the legal limit—and fourteen in the back seat. He ticketed the driver, Salvador Caban, forty-seven, who had only one arm.

....

NEW YORK CITY POLICE AR-

rested three men in the shooting death of a cocaine dealer, including Domingo Osario, twenty-two, whom they accused of driving the getaway car—even though he has no arms.

....

LILY FOWLER, EIGHTY, ENTERED

an automatic car wash at a service station in Richmond, California, but instead of braking she hit the accelerator. "I just shot through the car wash like a bullet," she said. "The car was going so fast I couldn't think how to shut it off." Desperately reaching for the brake pedal, she kept hitting the accelerator and headed for the street, where she slammed into a passing car. She then turned into a driveway leading back to the station and mowed down a gas pump, causing an explosion that engulfed three other cars and her own in flames, then hit a Volvo before slamming to a stop against the concrete wall of the car wash. She said it was her first accident in sixty years of driving.

···

SUSPENDING KENNETH WOR-
les's driver's license after his sixth arrest for driving under the influence didn't keep the Naples, Florida, man off the road. Police arrested him again for drunken driving when he ran a red light at a busy intersection while riding his ten-horsepower lawn mower.

···

CAIRO ALMOST TURNED INTO A
battleground in 1985 as private cars became billboards for clashing religious slogans. Automobiles owned by Muslims carried bumper stickers announcing, "There is no God but Allah, and Mohammed is His prophet." Christian cars countered with bumper stickers depicting Christ on the cross and the Virgin Mary. The Egyptian government stepped in before the streets turned into a religious demolition derby by decreeing that drivers with such bumper stickers would forfeit their licenses for one year.

···

IN CANADA'S ALBERTA PROV-

ince, police stopped teenager David Zurfluh for erratic driving. When they put him in the back of their patrol car, he tried to eat his cotton undershorts. "We believed that he had swallowed the fabric on the theory that it would absorb alcohol before he was given a breath analysis test," Corporal Jim Mitchell said. Even though Zurfluh testified in court that indeed that had been his intention, the judge acquitted him because the breath test showed his blood alcohol level to be exactly at the legal limit.

LOST AND FOUND

•••••••••••••••••••••••••••••

IN OSLO, NORWAY, JERMUND

Skogstad, fifty, was moving into his new apartment
when he took a break to get something to eat. He
went to a nearby cafe but forgot to take his wallet,
which contained his new address. He was unable to
find his way home. "This is embarrassing," he told a
newspaper a month later, hoping word of his plight
would reach his new landlady, whom he had paid a
month's rent in advance.

••

ORNITHOLOGISTS WERE ELATED

by the 1990 sighting beside a road in Australia's
Queensland State of an elusive night parrot thought
to be extinct, having not been seen since 1912. Their
joy was tempered by the fact that the emerald-green

and yellow-spotted bird was found dead, the likely victim of a car's windshield.

. . . .

A DALLAS COUPLE, CHARLIE

and Sharon Reed, were happy enough when the police called to say their stolen car had been found. After they saw it, they were even happier. When it had been stolen three months earlier, the banana-yellow 1976 Volkswagen convertible had a cracked windshield and a smashed rear end. When the Reeds picked up the car, it had new bumpers, new fenders, a new paint job, and a new windshield. It even had a full tank of gas. "I think the thieves aligned the front end, too," Charlie Reed said.

. . . .

BEFORE HIS ARREST IN OCTOBER

1989 in Jefferson, Texas, animal trainer Arlan Seidon spent five years as a fugitive. He managed to elude authorities despite having to conceal two full-grown elephants that he had with him the whole time. He also had to secretly acquire six hundred pounds of food a day and dispose of five hundred pounds of droppings. The sixty-year-old man and the elephants— which he raised, then sold to a man in New Jersey, kidnapped to rescue from abuse, and refused a court order to return to their owner—spent their first four years moving around the northern United States and Canada before fleeing to Texas. Seidon took the elephants to Florida each winter, traveling when weigh

scales weren't open and on back roads. He also wore
disguises and used a pseudonym.

....

THE FRANCISCAN MONASTERY IN

Kennebunkport, Maine, reported in 1988 that the remains of Saint Anthony were missing from the mon-
astery chapel. Saint Anthony is the saint of lost articles.

....

A TWENTY-THREE-MONTH-OLD

child riding in the back seat of an eleven-year-old
automobile apparently reached down to get a potato
chip and slipped through a hole in the floor. According to Springfield, Illinois, police, the car's driver and
the boy's mother didn't realize the child was missing
until the car reached a stoplight. He was found and
not seriously injured.

....

A TIME CAPSULE BURIED IN WIL-

kinsburg, Pennsylvania, in 1962 was scheduled to be
opened in 1986 as part of the community's hundredth
anniversary celebration. Nobody could find the stain-
less-steel box, however, because all those who knew
where it was buried had died. Harold J. Ake, eighty-
seven, who was a member of the Wilkinsburg Cham-
ber of Commerce in 1962, recalled that the City Council held a special closed meeting to decide where to

bury the capsule but feared vandals would dig it up, so "they didn't tell anyone."

That same year, District of Columbia officials needed to use a computer that tracks master financial accounts for the nation's capital but couldn't because no one knew the password. It had been changed by Alvin Frost, thirty-eight, a cash management analyst, who said he forgot what it was, although he recalled that it had something to do with the Declaration of Independence.

....

IN RENTON, WASHINGTON, TAN-

na Barney, twenty-four, concerned that her husband Marc was overdue on a long motorcycle trip, went looking for him in the family car. According to state police, as she rounded a curve she hit him head-on and killed him.

....

WHEN HIS WIFE DIED IN 1981,

Robert Valentine of New Bremen, Ohio, decided to donate her brain to medical research. The brain, which was sent to Strong Memorial Hospital in Rochester, New York, never arrived. After a search by the U.S. Postal Service and United Parcel Service failed to locate the package, Valentine sued the hospital that was supposed to have sent it.

In Gainesville, Florida, two seventh-grade boys waiting for a school bus found a human brain on the ground and decided to take it to school. "I didn't know what else to do with it," said Allen Ricks, fourteen.

The other boy, Adaryll Lee, fourteen, said he "thought somebody had been killed and the brain had been left behind." Authorities found no evidence of foul play, however, and said the brain was "an anatomic specimen that was professionally removed."

....

IN EL PASO, TEXAS, DRUG EN-

forcement Administration agent David M. Petz was making a last-minute check of the home he was selling when he found some boxes the buyer had stashed in a closet. They contained 415 pounds of cocaine. DEA agents arrested the new owner and four other men, who were part of a drug ring the DEA had been trying to nab for a while.

....

PROBLEMS OF
DEMOCRACY
· ·

IN ALEXANDRIA, VIRGINIA,
Mayor James P. Moran's congressional election campaign organization charged that a high-ranking aide
to the mayor had her garbage removed several times
in the middle of the night and replaced with "fake
garbage." Fund-raiser Linda Biles reported that twice
after putting her garbage out for collection, she saw a
well-dressed man "take her garbage bags and replace
them then drive away." Moran said Biles knew the
trash was switched because her trash was in green
bags and the replacement bags were yellow.

· ·

CLAUDE CONTAMINE, FORMER
managing director of the French state television channel Antenne 2, was accused in court of brainwashing
the electorate into voting for President Francois

Mitterrand in 1988. Accusers told the court the channel had improperly used subliminal advertising techniques on the nightly evening news to enhance Mitterrand's impact on the voters, charging his picture appeared on the screen for a split second ten times each night during the introduction to the evening news. Robert Casanovas, a legal expert who brought the court action against Contamine, said, "I voted for Mitterrand in the first round of the election because I was influenced by these images."

....

BOSTON CITY COUNCILOR

Brian J. McLaughlin lost the election for council president by one vote—his own. Even though his fellow liberals on the thirteen-member council offered McLaughlin their support, he honored a commitment he had previously made to vote for conservative Christopher Ianella, who won.

....

MORE THAN ONE THOUSAND

male employees of the Indian government paraded in their underwear around New Delhi in 1983 to protest the poor quality of their homespun uniforms, which they were directed to wear to honor the wishes of Mohandas K. Gandhi. The workers demanded new polyester-and-polished-cotton clothing.

In Cartagena, Colombia, in 1985, about one thousand dock workers reported for duty in their underwear to protest a pay boost of only 10 percent and the suspension of their clothing allowance.

203

Three years later, two Dutch police officers in Rotterdam, one male and one female, took center field during halftime of a soccer game and removed their clothes to protest wages and working conditions.

··

TO CELEBRATE THE TWO HUN-

dredth birthday of the U.S. Constitution, El Segundo, California, City Councilman Alan West was supposed to give a proclamation to Elaine Hunter, a representative of the local chapter of the Daughters of the American Revolution. West strayed from a prepared statement, however, and began a lengthy talk on his "favorite bill in the Bill of Rights"—the Fifth Amendment, which protects private property. West's delivery apparently moved his colleagues so much that the council proceeded with its business, forgetting about giving Hunter her proclamation until someone suddenly remembered a half-hour later during a public hearing on weed abatement.

··

RICARDO SANCHEZ, THE MAYOR

of Maicolpue, Chile, was making a speech when hecklers began shouting antigovernment slogans at him, whereupon he collapsed and died of a heart attack.

··

AFTER THE GROUP AMERICANS

for a Competent Federal Judicial System claimed responsibility for bombings that killed a federal judge and a lawyer, Ku Klux Klan Grand Wizard Thom Robb accused the group of trying to give the KKK and other racist organizations a bad name.

Following the 1977 showing of the television special *Roots,* the KKK requested equal time to present a rebuttal. *"Roots* was a biased historical presentation from a black militant point of view," said the Klan's national grand dragon, David Duke. ABC-TV denied the request.

....

AT LEAST EIGHTY OFFICIALS AND

civic leaders in San Francisco reported receiving packages containing used men's underwear and photographs of a white-haired man's rear end.

....

OPPORTUNITY
KNOCKS

• •

FRANCISCO MARINO, A MEXICAN
citizen who had been in the United States for six
months working as a dishwasher, was hit by a New
York City subway train and lost an arm when he fell
drunk onto the tracks. He sued the Transit Authority,
arguing he wouldn't have fallen on the track if transit
officials had removed him from the platform after
observing that he was intoxicated. After a jury awarded
him $9.3 million, Marino exclaimed, "God Bless
America."

• •

WHEN CUSTOMERS COMPLAINED
that a slot machine at a Laundromat in Anchorage,
Alaska, was a fraud because it was fixed not to pay
off, the authorities disagreed. They said the no-payoff
feature was what made the machine legal. If the cus-

tomers could have won, the machine would have been a gambling device, which is illegal in Alaska.

·······································

NINE THOUSAND HUMAN EM-

bryos are stockpiled in the nation's freezers, according to a 1989 report by the *San Francisco Examiner*. The newspaper noted that other nations also are freezing embryos, including Australia, where the world's first test-tube orphans are stored. Those embryos were created in 1981, then lost their mother and her husband in a plane crash in South America. If successfully implanted and born, they would inherit the couple's multimillion-dollar estate.

·······································

DESPITE THE LACK OF SCIEN-

tific proof that the Loch Ness monster exists, it generates $42 million a year in revenue from tourists who visit the Scottish lake each year hoping to see the legendary creature. Mackay Consultants of Inverness also pointed out the monster myth creates about 2,500 jobs.

·······································

A DRUG COUNSELOR IN PHILA-

delphia was arrested for offering an abuser on probation a drug-free sample of urine in exchange for a Mercedes. The nineteen-year-old abuser, facing a jail term because of his tainted urine, thought the price was too steep and told his lawyer, who notified the district attorney's office. Investigators provided the nineteen-year-old with a $28,000 Mercedes for the deal, then arrested thirty-six-year-old David Holland after he signed the title and accepted the keys to the car.

POLICE IN BATON ROUGE, LOUI-

siana, arrested Thomas Hoffmann, thirty-five, for ordering about $200,000 worth of mail-order merchandise—up to fifty boxes a day—and not paying the bills. According to Sergeant Randy Crowe, Hoffmann used five post office boxes and 227 aliases to receive the catalog merchandise. Police recovered enough goods from his home and two storage rooms to fill an eight-thousand-square-foot warehouse, where sixteen officers spent six hours sorting through the orders so they could be returned. Among them were books, magazines, clothes, porcelain plates, globes, videotapes, and more than six-hundred compact discs. Crowe said Hoffmann "told us this was kind of something that snowballed on him."

THE CITY COUNCIL OF HAMIL-

ton, Ohio, voted 5 to 1 to add an exclamation mark to the town's official name to attract attention and possibly new industry and jobs.

TALK SHOW HOST JOAN RIVERS

was walking down a Manhattan street in 1989 when

she saw a woman arguing with a tow truck driver who had already driven a block with the woman's car. Rivers intervened and persuaded the truck driver to unhook the car. In gratitude, the woman, a therapist who happened to host a cable television show called *Money and Emotions,* agreed to participate in a planned Rivers show about faking orgasms.

....

WHEN BOSTON UNIVERSITY AN-
nounced in 1989 that it was considering a plan to raise money by taking out life insurance policies on its students, both insurance experts and students expressed their doubts about the plan. The insurance people said the plan wouldn't work, whereas David Vogel, editor of the student newspaper, pointed out "a disaster like Pan Am Flight 103 going down with a bunch of BU students on board could be considered a financial boon for Boston University."

....

CAPTIVE
AUDIENCES

KENNETH OUTLAND, TWENTY-
one, manager of a Domino's Pizza in Hemet, California, easily escaped after a robber left him handcuffed
inside a freezer. Outland said he recognized the
manacles as a cheap pair of novelty cuffs like ones he
had bought five years earlier on a high school field
trip in Tijuana, Mexico, and simply used the key
from them that he just happened always to carry with
him.

Less well-prepared was Albert Moore, a cigarette
salesman who was robbed in Houston and left handcuffed by thieves who made off with his cigarette-
filled van. Moore spent an hour pleading with motorists
and passersby to come to his aid, but most, apparently thinking he was an escaped prisoner, ignored
him or fled. Finally, police, responding to calls of a
handcuffed man, freed Moore.

AFTER BEING TAKEN HOSTAGE IN

her New York City apartment, Ruth Wolko, eighty-four, mothered her twenty-nine-year-old captor into releasing her. The five-and-a-half-hour standoff began when Jose Cruz broke into Wolko's apartment while escaping police after being caught breaking into another apartment. Wolko, described by neighbor Elsie Hyman as "the classic Jewish mother," calmed her captor with offerings from her refrigerator and sincere concern about his predicament, including urging him to find a legitimate job. Cruz finally told police he was willing to trade Wolko for two cigarettes.

....

TAIWAN'S JUSTICE MINISTRY

proposed that condemned prisoners who agreed to donate organs after death be spared the traditional execution (being placed face down in a sandpit and shot through the heart). Instead, they could elect to be executed by a bullet in the head.

....

POLICE INVESTIGATING A RE-

port of a light in an alley behind a home in Cheverly, Maryland, found a city-owned camera aimed at the home's second-floor bathroom. They questioned a fifty-eight-year-old neighbor who had access to the camera and found 191 videotapes, at least 10 of which showed people in the neighborhood using their bathrooms.

....

AFTER RECEIVING REPORTS

that William and Marika Runnells, awaiting trial for ninety-eight fraud and racketeering charges, were hypnotizing other inmates and possibly even jailers at the Virginia Beach, Virginia, city jail, Sheriff Frank Drew ordered the couple to stop. "I heard they were playing games with the staff," Drew said, "and I just wanted to break it up before it got out of hand." The Runnellses explained they were just trying to help them stop smoking.

....

IN SACRAMENTO, CALIFORNIA,

Cathy Baillargeon won a $12,000 settlement in her lawsuit claiming that she was sitting on the toilet in the restroom of the Black Angus restaurant when KROY radio disc jockey Dan Walker kicked open the stall door and placed a microphone in front of her face to record her screams for broadcast.

And in Slidell, Louisiana, police arrested Jimmy Clarence Spiess, fifty-three, for bugging the women's restrooms of a bar below his apartment.

....

AFTER FIVE PASSERSBY TURNED

down his polite request that they help unload his girlfriend's furniture from a truck and carry it into her house, Barry Andrews, thirty-nine, of Brodheadsville, Pennsylvania, pulled a gun on others who walked by. He was arrested for assault and making terroristic threats, as well as indecent exposure since, according to the police report, at some point during the incident he removed his clothes.

···

FOUR STUDENTS OF FINLAND'S

National Theatre School staged an avant-garde nude show in which they pelted the audience with fireworks and human excrement, sprayed them with stolen fire extinguishers, and, for their grand finale, chased them out of the theater with whips. After a court decided the performance was not art, the students were given a suspended sentence for assault and jeopardizing public health and fined $50,000.

···

IN DEERFIELD, FLORIDA, BROW-

ard County Circuit Judge Lawrence Korda sentenced Philip Tiger, seventy-seven, who was convicted of manslaughter for stabbing his wife to death and who tried to take his own life, to watch the movie *It's a Wonderful Life*.

···

ART COLLECTOR ETHEL SCULL,

sixty-seven, was fined $1,000 after pleading guilty to making 1,208 telephone calls in one week in January 1988 to her financial adviser, Charles Lewis. She made the calls—485 in one day—to complain that she lost money in the October 19, 1987, stock market crash as a result of his bad advice. In reality, she had made $300,000.

••

IDENTITY
CRISIS

●●●●●●●●●●●●●●●●●●●●●●●●●●●●●●●●●●

AFTER A SEX-CHANGE OPERA-

tion in May 1982, Christine Lynne Oliver of Minneapolis began having second thoughts. "I started getting feelings that my old male identity was returning," she said after reverting to wearing short hair and pants. "It's like waking up from a bad dream or something."

That November, she filed a $50,000 suit against four doctors and the hospital, claiming they never should have allowed the operation in the first place. She said they failed to conduct a thorough enough psychological exam, which would have shown she wasn't really a woman trapped in a man's body, just a guy having problems getting over the death of his wife.

●●

HIGH SCHOOL ADMINISTRATORS

in Edwardsville, Illinois, discovered that a twelfth-grader who told them when he enrolled that he had lost his parents in an auto accident and had been recruited to play football at the University of Southern California was actually a twenty-five-year-old army deserter wanted for larceny. "He looked like a seventeen- or eighteen-year-old," principal Lawrence Busch said of 6-foot-4, 210-pound Doyle R. McMahan. "He dressed just like the other kids."

In Colorado Springs, Colorado, high school officials discovered that a 5-foot-9, 164-pound eleventh-grade cheerleader was actually a twenty-six-year-old female impersonator with a criminal record for burglary and theft. Charles Daugherty enrolled at Coronado High School as Cheyen Weatherly, claiming to have studied in Greece under a private tutor. He performed with the cheerleading squad twice and sang soprano in the school choir. Several football players expressed interest in dating the newest cheerleader before Daugherty was discovered and pleaded guilty to criminal impersonation.

....

JEFFREY ALLEN HAYES, THIRTY-

two, pleaded guilty to strangling Shannon Fay Stevens in West Seattle, Washington, explaining he mistook her for his ex-girlfriend, Barbara Dodge.

....

PRINCE GEORGE'S COUNTY,

Maryland, police conducting a strip-search of L. A. Bowie, who claimed to be the father of two robbery and murder suspects and was arrested in connection with their crimes, were unable to decide whether the bearded Bowie was a man or a woman. Doctors at the county jail decided to house Bowie as a woman until police could determine whether Bowie is the boys' biological father or their mother.

At the trial of one of the sons, defense attorneys tried to show that his upbringing made him psychologically unstable. L. A.—formerly Linda Anne—Bowie was a key witness, testifying that his son used to call him "Ma," but when he was about ten years old started calling him "Pa."

....

POLICE IN WAPPINGERS FALLS,

New York, arrested twenty-year-old Nicholas Sucich, who they said had a mental problem that caused him to be different characters. They charged him with giving at least one person a tetanus-type shot in the rear end while imagining he was a doctor. After reading of his arrest, several people called the police to report that Sucich may also have injected them. Police who searched his apartment found one hundred milliliters of the drug Xylocaine and eight hundred hypodermic needles.

....

LESS THAN A MONTH AFTER CHI-

cago aldermen unexpectedly and unanimously passed a resolution to honor slain Black Panther leader Fred Hampton, seventeen of the aldermen, all white, withdrew their names and urged that the measure be rescinded. One of them, Edward Burke, explained

217

that some aldermen weren't paying attention to the measure and thought they had been voting to honor Chicago Bears lineman Dan Hampton.

....

A MAN WHO THREATENED TO

sue himself for negligence did not have to pay tax on his $122,500 settlement, according to U.S. Tax Court Judge Robert Ruwe. The case began when Peter Maxwell was owner of a urethane foam padding manufacturing business in Chino, California, and also a paid employee of the company. After suffering severe injuries when a protruding bolt on a mixing device snagged his sweater and pulled him into the whirling machinery, Maxwell the employee hired an attorney to sue himself as owner of the company. Maxwell the owner hired another attorney to defend the firm.

Without going to court, the two attorneys agreed that Maxwell the owner had been negligent in allowing the bolt to protrude and should pay Maxwell the employee $122,500 as compensation. Although federal tax law let Maxwell have the money tax-free and let the company deduct the amount as a business expense, the Internal Revenue Service viewed the deal suspiciously and billed Maxwell the employee for $64,000 in income taxes on the payment and Maxwell the owner for $58,000 because of the loss of a deduction. Both Maxwells appealed, and Ruwe ruled against the IRS.

....

AFTER SUFFERING A STROKE, A

thirty-two-year-old Baltimore man suddenly began

speaking with a Scandinavian accent, according to neurophysiologist Dr. Dean Tippett of the University of Maryland School of Medicine. Tippet said the man had no experience with foreign languages and seemed to enjoy his new accent, saying he hoped it would help attract women. It faded six weeks after the stroke.

....

WALTER MURPHY, TWENTY-

seven, suffocated after burrowing into the hole beneath a concrete slab in his backyard in Los Angeles in September 1982. Police said he apparently believed he was a gopher. His mother, Olga Davis, explained that her son had first started digging holes in April, staying in them for up to two weeks at a time. "Last July, they dug him out of the same hole," she said. "I know he was depressed. He couldn't get a job."

....

UNCATEGORI-
CALLY WEIRD
• •

A SERIAL KILLER KNOWN ONLY as "Stoneman" stalks the streets of Calcutta at night, killing his victims, the street dwellers of that city, by dropping a thirty- to fifty-pound slab of concrete on their heads as they sleep. Despite the fact that over one million people live on Calcutta's streets, there have been no witnesses to the eleven (as of March 1990) reported murders.

• •

SPEAKING BEFORE A GROUP OF business executives, Domino's Pizza founder Thomas Monaghan, whose estimated worth exceeds $500 million, said, "To me one of the most exciting things in the world is being poor." He then went on to explain how a family of four could live on $68 a year. He also

220

recommended buying a house trailer to live in—"my gosh, that was the greatest living I ever did."

....

SOVIET PSYCHIC E. FRENKEL

failed in his attempt to stop an oncoming freight train through the use of his psychic powers. The train engineer said that Frenkel jumped onto the tracks in front of the train with his arms raised and his head lowered. Investigators found Frenkel's notes, which read, "First I stopped a bicycle, cars, and a streetcar. Now I'm going to stop a train."

....

BOSTON PSYCHIATRIST SHEL-

don Zigelbaum, accused of sexually abusing four female patients, was also charged by the Massachusetts state licensing board with asking the husband of one of them for a $6,000 loan so he could defend himself against the allegations.

In another case, after pleading guilty to embezzling $95,000 from the bank she worked at, Susan Nuckols, thirty-four, of Shady Side, Maryland, avoided a jail sentence by repaying the amount she stole with money she borrowed from the same bank.

....

NIGHT AFTER NIGHT FOR SEV-

eral months, a San Antonio, Texas, homeowner told a

court, a group of men drove up to his house to throw used tires into his yard until there were about ten thousand of them stacked eight feet high. Johnny Crawford, fifty-seven, testified that whenever he tried to stop the men, they beat him up.

OFFICIALS IN ORIVESI, FINLAND,

investigating an outbreak of illness affecting hundreds, possibly thousands, of people traced it to dozens of pantyhose, which they found blocking the city's sewers, causing them to overflow and contaminate drinking water. Construction engineer Heikki Seppala said, "It looked like someone had deliberately stuffed a whole year's supply of tights into the pipes."

....

RESIDENTS OF A MOBILE HOME

park near Brandon, Florida, were pinned down for nearly two hours by gunfire. Police who investigated also had to dodge bullets before discovering the shots were coming from two out-of-town businessmen making a law-enforcement training video at a private firing range one and a half miles away. They were testing an M-16 rifle, a 9mm Heckler, and a Koch MP5 assault weapon.

....

WHEN MICHAEL WEST, TWENTY-

nine, used a toy gun to try to rob Eddie Nassar, seventy-six, in Rochester, New York, Nassar's seventy-two-year-old wife Freida pulled out her own toy gun and pointed it at the robber, who pleaded with Freida not to shoot. As West started to run away, a neighbor who had heard the commotion threw a baseball bat at West, knocking him to the ground. He got up and continued running, but police were able to follow the trail of blood dripping from the wound on his head and arrest him.

....

BETWEEN 1980 AND 1984, 136

fatalities in North Carolina were attributed to "Lying-in-the-Road" death. Dr. Lawrence S. Harris, a state medical examiner who studied the phenomenon, explained that the victims were intoxicated individuals who, while walking home at night, would lie down on warm rural roads and fall asleep. During the same five-year period, Tennessee recorded 31 such deaths, while Georgia saw 21 in 1985 and 1986, and Arizona had 13 in 1984.

....

AFTER HAVING BEEN STRUCK BY

a hit-and-run driver as he walked along Interstate 5 near San Diego, Juan Francisco Camacho spent four days on the highway median strip signaling for help as an estimated half-million cars passed him. During the next few days, Camacho, in great pain and often delirious, sat up and even managed to stand in full view of people at nearby businesses.

....

CHINA GAVE COMMEMORATIVE

gold watches to the soldiers who participated in crushing the 1989 democracy movement in Tiananmen Square. The watch face features a soldier on sentry duty, while an inscription says "Commemoration of the June 1989 crackdown."

....

FRANCISCO MACIAS NGUEMA,

dictator of Equatorial Guinea from 1968 to 1979, once staged a hanging of his enemies in the public square of the capital, Malabo, while playing the song "Those Were the Days" over loudspeakers. He executed ten of the original eleven members of his cabinet and even ordered the death of the vice president because his copy of Macias's official portrait was torn.

SOURCES

Agence France-Press
Archives of Dermatology
The Argus (Rock Island, Illinois)
Arkansas Gazette (Little Rock)
Asbury Park Press (New Jersey)
The Asheville Citizen (North Carolina)
Associated Press
The Athens Messenger (Ohio)
Austin American-Statesman (Texas)
The Birmingham News (Alabama)
The Blade (Toledo, Ohio)
The Boston Globe
California Lawyer
The Capital (Annapolis, Maryland)
The Charlotte Observer (North Carolina)
Chicago Tribune
Chillicothe Gazette (Ohio)
Chronicle of Higher Education

The Columbus Dispatch (Ohio)
The Commercial Appeal (Memphis, Tennessee)
Cook's Magazine
The Courier-Journal (Louisville, Kentucky)
The Daily Oklahoman (Oklahoma City)
Daily Texan (University of Texas at Austin)
The Dallas Morning News
Dallas Times Herald
Dayton Daily News (Ohio)
The Des Moines Register (Iowa)
Detroit Free Press
Deutsche-Presse-Agentur
The Economist
Editor & Publisher
The Edmonton Journal (Alberta)
The El Paso Times (Texas)
The Evening Sun (Baltimore, Maryland)
The Evening Telegram (Superior, Wisconsin)
Federal Reporter (2nd Series)
Fortune
Freethought Today
Gainesville Sun (Florida)
Gannett News Service
The Globe and Mail (Toronto)
Greensboro News & Record (North Carolina)
Hammacher Schlemmer Catalog
Herald-Citizen (Cookeville, Tennessee)
Houston Chronicle
The Houston Post
The Idaho Statesman (Boise)
The International Herald Tribune
Journal and Constitution (Atlanta)
Journal of the American Medical Association
Journal of Nervous Medical Disorders

The Kansas City Star (Missouri)
The Knoxville News-Sentinel (Tennessee)
Lexington Herald-Leader (Kentucky)
Los Angeles Times
The Miami Herald
The Milwaukee Journal
Milwaukee Sentinel
Multinational Environmental Outlook
Naples Daily News (Florida)
Nashville Banner (Tennessee)
New Hampshire Sunday News (Manchester)
New Haven Register (Connecticut)
New York Daily News
New York Post
The New York Times
News-Pilot (San Pedro, California)
The News-Sentinel (Fort Wayne, Indiana)
Newsweek
The Olympian (Olympia, Washington)
The Oregonian (Portland)
The Orlando Sentinel (Florida)
Pacific Reporter (2nd Series)
The Palm Beach Post (West Palm Beach, Florida)
People Weekly
Philadelphia Daily News
The Philadelphia Inquirer
The Pittsburgh Press
The Plain Dealer (Cleveland)
Portland Press-Herald (Maine)
The Post-Standard (Syracuse, New York)
Progressive Grocer
Public Opinion (Chambersburg, Pennsylvania)
The Record (Bergen County, New Jersey)
Reuters

Richmond Times-Dispatch (Virginia)
Roanoke Times (Virginia)
Rocky Mountain News (Denver)
Saginaw News (Michigan)
St. Louis Post-Dispatch
St. Paul Pioneer Press & Dispatch (Minnesota)
St. Petersburg Times (Florida)
Salt Lake Tribune (Salt Lake City, Utah)
San Francisco Chronicle
San Francisco Examiner
San Jose Mercury News (California)
San Luis Obispo County Telegram-Tribune (California)
Santa Barbara News-Press (California)
The Sault Star (Sault Ste. Marie, Ontario)
The Scranton Times (Pennsylvania)
Seattle Post-Intelligencer
The Seattle Times
The Star-Ledger (Newark, New Jersey)
Star-News (Pasadena, California)
Star-Phoenix (Saskatoon, Saskatchewan)
Star-Tribune (Minneapolis)
The Sun (Baltimore, Maryland)
Sun-Sentinel (Fort Lauderdale, Florida)
Sunday Times (London, England)
Syracuse Herald American (New York)
Syracuse Herald-Journal (New York)
Syracuse New Times (New York)
Tampa Tribune (Florida)
The Tennessean (Nashville)
Time
The Times-Picayune (New Orleans)
Times-Union (Rochester, New York)
Topeka Capital-Journal (Kansas)
The Toronto Star

The Toronto Sun
The Tribune (Oakland, California)
United Press International
USA Today
The Virginian-Pilot (Norfolk, Virginia)
The Wall Street Journal
The Washington Monthly
The Washington Post
The Washington Times
The Wichita Eagle-Beacon (Kansas)
The Wilkes-Barre Times Leader (Pennsylvania)